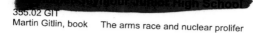

DATE DUE

		PRINTED IN U.S.A.

The Arms Race and Nuclear Proliferation

Other Books of Related Interest

At Issue Series

Biological and Chemical Weapons
Nuclear Weapons
Weapons of War

Current Controversies Series

The Arms Trade
Nuclear Armament

Opposing Viewpoints Series

Biological Warfare
Bioterrorism
Doomsday Scenarios
National Security
Nuclear Power

VIEWPOINTS ON
MODERN WORLD HISTORY

The Arms Race and Nuclear Proliferation

Martin Gitlin, Book Editor

GREENHAVEN
PUBLISHING

Published in 2018 by Greenhaven Publishing, LLC
353 3rd Avenue, Suite 255, New York, NY 10010

Copyright © 2018 by Greenhaven Publishing, LLC

First Edition

Articles in Greenhaven Publishing anthologies are often edited for length to meet page
requirements. In addition, original titles of these works are changed to clearly present
the main thesis and to explicitly indicate the author's opinion. Every effort is made to
ensure that Greenhaven Publishing accurately reflects the original intent of the authors.
Every effort has been made to trace the owners of the copyrighted material.

Cover image: Michael Dunning/Photographer's Choice/Getty Images.

Library of Congress Cataloging-in-Publication Data

Names: Gitlin, Martin, editor.
Title: The arms race and nuclear proliferation / Martin Gitlin, book editor.
Description: New York : Greenhaven Publishing, [2018] | Series: Viewpoints on modern
world history | Includes bibliographical references and index. | Audience: Grades 9–12.
Identifiers: LCCN 2017028946 | ISBN 9781534501379 (library bound)
Subjects: LCSH: Nuclear weapons—Juvenile literature. | Arms race—
Juvenile literature. | Nuclear nonproliferation—Juvenile literature.
Classification: LCC U264 .A76 2018 | DDC 355.02/17—dc23
LC record available at https://lccn.loc.gov/2017028946

Manufactured in the United States of America

Website: http://greenhavenpublishing.com

Contents

Chapter 1: A Blast from the Past and Later Threats

Nuclear armament came from superpowers clashing during the Cold War era. Why then, twenty years after the Cold War's end, are nations still depending on nuclear weapons and the nuclear threat?

Chapter 2: The Major Players in a Deadly Game

Chapter 3: Planning a Peaceful Future

Foreword

"The more we know about the past enables us to ask richer and more provocative questions about who we are today. We also must tell the next generation one of the great truths of history: that no past event was preordained. Every battle, every election, and revolution could have turned out differently at any point along the way, just as a person's own life can change unpredictably."

—David McCullough, American historian

History is punctuated by momentous events—turning points for the nations involved, with impacts felt far beyond their borders. Displaying the full range of human capabilities—from violence, greed, and ignorance to heroism, courage, and strength—they are nearly always complicated and multifaceted. Any student of history faces the challenge of grasping both the broader elements and the nuances of world-changing events, such as wars, social movements, and environmental disasters. Textbooks offer only so much help, burdened as they are by constraints of length and single-perspective narratives. True understanding of history's significant events comes from exposure to a variety of perspectives from the people involved intimately, as well as those observing from a distance of miles or years.

Viewpoints on Modern World History examines global events from the twentieth century onward, presenting analysis and observation from numerous vantage points. The series offers high school, early college level, and general interest readers a thematically arranged anthology of previously published materials that address a major historical event or period. Each volume opens with background information on the event, presents the controversies surrounding the event, and concludes with the implications and legacy of the event. By providing a variety of perspectives, this series can be used to inform debate, help develop critical thinking skills, increase global awareness, and enhance an understanding of international viewpoints on history.

Material in each volume is selected from a diverse range of sources. Articles taken from these sources are carefully edited and introduced to provide context and background.

Each volume in the Viewpoints on Modern World History series also includes:

- An annotated **table of contents** that provides a brief summary of each essay in the volume
- An **introduction** specific to the volume topic
- A **chapter preface** setting up the chapter content and providing historical context
- For each viewpoint, a brief **introduction** that has notes about the author and source of the viewpoint and provides a summary of its main points
- Informational **sidebars** that explore the lives of key individuals, give background on historical events, or explain scientific or technical concepts
- A **chronology** of dates important to the period
- A **bibliography** of additional books, periodicals, and websites for further research
- A **subject index** that offers links to people, places, and events cited in the text

Viewpoints on Modern World History is designed for a broad spectrum of readers who want to learn more about not only history but also current events, political science, government, international relations, and sociology. This includes students doing research for class assignments or debates, teachers and faculty seeking to supplement course materials, and others wanting to improve their understanding of history. The volumes in this series are designed to illuminate a complicated event, to spark debate, and to show the human perspective behind the world's most significant happenings of recent decades.

Introduction

> *"Today, every inhabitant of this planet must contemplate the day when this planet may no longer be habitable. Every man, woman and child lives under a nuclear sword of Damocles, hanging by the slenderest of threads, capable of being cut at any moment by accident or miscalculation or by madness. The weapons of war must be abolished before they abolish us."*
>
> *- President John F. Kennedy to the General Assembly of the United Nations in 1961*

Pandora's Box was opened on August 6, 1945. The demons had been let loose, never to be returned.

That was the date an American plane called the *Enola Gay* unloaded the first of two atomic bombs on Japan to force that country to surrender and finally put an end to the nightmare that was World War II. The righteousness and strategic viability of unleashing the deadliest weapon in human history on the cities of Hiroshima and Nagasaki (three days later) has been debated ever since, but many argue that an invasion of Japan would have resulted in more deaths than the bombs themselves.

The issue quickly became not whether the atomic bombs should have been dropped on Japan, but how mankind could survive the invention of a weapon with the capability of destroying the earth. And when the Soviet Union successfully detonated one in 1949 to launch the arms race, the Cold War became far more frightening.

And the more the world has changed, the more it has remained the same. The Soviet Union is now Russia, but the good tidings that followed its conversion and the freedom of the Eastern European countries it once controlled has dissipated as that country has flexed its military muscles once again. Many other countries, such as China, Pakistan, Israel, and India, have become nuclear capable. And even scarier is that rogue nations such as Iran and North Korea, controlled by terrifying leaders that have threatened to use whatever military power at their disposal, have worked to build weapons that could wipe out millions in a matter of minutes.

The arms race and nuclear proliferation have motivated many different opinions on how best to ensure no such bombs are ever dropped upon the earth. Mankind has been fortunate thus far in that the one dropped on Nagasaki more than seventy years ago has remained the last. That fact has supported the view, at least to its adherents, that ownership of nuclear weapons is the greatest deterrent to their use. The notion that no country will be bold enough to launch a missile strike when it understands that it too will be destroyed has its merits.

That argument remains valid even when one considers successful efforts to lessen nuclear stockpiles in the United States and the former Soviet Union. One can claim that only the elimination of nuclear weapons through negotiation and verification can end the threat. After all, what is the difference if the Russians can wipe out America thirty times over instead of seventy and vice versa?

Yet the very threat of nuclear war has generally resulted in cooler heads prevailing. The closest the world ever came to such a terrifying exchange occurred during the Cuban Missile Crisis in 1962. The event that had the world on edge resulted from the Soviets placing missiles in short range of major US cities. Disaster was averted when the Americans agreed to remove their weapons from Turkey if the Soviets agreed to dismantle their program in Cuba. The sigh of relief could be heard around the globe.

Science might eventually end the fears. Some gained hope in the 1980s, when American president Ronald Reagan suggested that a "Star War" shield could eventually be created that would block nuclear weapons from reaching their intended destination. He even claimed that he would share that technology with the Soviets. It seems nobody knows for certain if such a breakthrough is forthcoming or even possible, but science remains unstoppable in its vision and marches forward to learn and solve problems. And, after all, there is no more significant problem on earth than the threat to its very existence through nuclear war.

That problem, however, no longer revolves around a conceivable war between major global powers such as the United States and Russia. Nuclear knowledge and capability in the hands of unstable dictators have grown into far greater threats. Saber-rattling world leaders such as Kim Jong-un, who seemingly cares nothing about the North Korean people he ruthlessly governs, has worked tirelessly and shamelessly to build a nuclear program while many among his citizenry starve.

The debate in regard to rogue nations such as Iran and North Korea joining the nuclear community is whether the antidote lies in negotiation or military strikes. China, which holds great influence over North Korea, has suggested that launching negotiations with that country could prevent it from launching missiles. But others believe that North Korea is hopelessly bent on furthering its nuclear ambitions and the only way to destroy it is to physically destroy it. The counter argument is that attacking the North Korean program would enrage the Chinese, thereby weakening the prospects of world peace.

An agreement with Iran to curb its program has served as a blueprint for the relative worthiness of negotiations in controlling a burgeoning nuclear power. Many have lambasted the United States and other countries for negotiating with a nation with a terrible human rights record and that has called for the elimination of Israel. The other side asks what other choice was available in claiming that, short of war, only by reaching a deal could it be possible to prevent Iran from gaining nuclear capability. Some feel, however, that the agreement will not achieve that goal.

Idealists assert that only the creation of a world government can save the world from destruction.

That view, too, has its merits. A world without borders would not be a planet without differences, and factions might be capable of attaining nuclear weapons, but the notion of the people of one planet being ruled by one government certainly lessens the threat of a nuclear exchange.

The issues are as complex as the world itself, and some of them are explored here in the pages of *Viewpoints on Modern World History: The Arms Race and Nuclear Proliferation.*

VIEWPOINTS ON
MODERN WORLD HISTORY

CHAPTER 1

A Blast from the Past and Later Threats

Preface

One cannot fully grasp the current and future state of the arms race and nuclear proliferation without an understanding of its past. That claim might be scoffed at given the fact that atomic weapons have been dropped on the face of the earth just twice— three days apart by the United States on Japan in August 1945 to end the bloodiest war ever waged. But the history of nuclear weapons and the impact they have had on the world extend far beyond the only incidents in which their frightening capabilities were shown in all their horror, thereby changing the specter of warfare and relations between nations forever.

The legendary offering from nineteenth- and twentieth-century philosopher and essayist George Santayana that those who fail to learn from history are condemned to repeat it is most appropriate in regard to this issue. But one must ask if world leaders have taken all the right steps to ensure that the Pandora's Box opened when the United States unleashed its fury to end World War II is never reopened. And should it have been opened in the first place? Arguments abound that a conventional invasion of Japan, given the plan of Russia to join the Pacific fray, would have cost far fewer lives than the propogandists have led us to believe.

The one terrifying incident that has given humankind insight into how desperately world leaders should work to avoid a nuclear exchange occurred during the Cuban Missile Crisis in October 1962. The most militant of American and Russian leaders called for strikes and counterstrikes that might have resulted in nuclear war and millions of deaths. But cooler heads prevailed, diplomacy defeated irrationality, compromise captured the day, and disaster was dodged.

Issues have since arisen that have tested resolve, patience, and intelligence. The nuclear threat seems to have at least been weakened among the major world powers. Though some believe stockpiles of weapons in countries such as the United States, Russia, and China mean that a high level of risk remains, current issues indicate that rogue nations with unstable leadership such as Iran and North Korea bring a far greater danger to the safety of the world.

The practicality of forging chancy diplomatic relations and deals with such countries, as the United States and others did with Iran, can be debated without resolution. Only time will tell which tact works best. But what remains clear is that world leaders and all peace-loving people must remain vigilant to make certain that the atomic bombs dropped on Hiroshima and Nagasaki continue to be the last that ever fall on the face of the earth. Given the increased magnitude of modern weaponry, the chance that humankind cannot survive an exchange is one that nobody can afford to take.

Bombing Hiroshima and Nagasaki Was a Mistake

Naji Dahi

Fullerton College professor Naji Dahi expresses a nontraditional viewpoint in the following piece, which was written for Anti Media. She argues that various factors show that both lives and the specter of nuclear war could have been saved if President Truman had rejected the idea of using the atomic bombs to subdue Japan in 1945. Dahi uses a variety of statistical data to dispute the claim of many experts and politicians of the era that potentially one million lives would have been lost had an invasion of the still-feisty nation been undertaken. Dahi even cites the views of some that neither an invasion nor the atomic strike was necessary to end the conflict against Japan.

August 6th and 9th of 2015 mark the 70th anniversary of the U.S. dropping two atomic bombs on Hiroshima and Nagasaki. This was the first and only time a state used a nuclear device on cities (or civilians) of another state. Some conservative estimates put the immediate death toll of the two bombs at 200,000 people. This is more than the total number of American soldiers killed in the Pacific front of World War II.

Since the bombs were dropped, the U.S. government, U.S. high school history texts, and the American public have asserted that dropping the bombs was necessary. According to one review of American textbooks by Satoshi Fujita, an assistant professor of U.S. modern history at Meiji University,

> *"...most of the textbooks published by the early 1980s carried the U.S. government's official view that the nuclear attacks allowed the U.S. troops to avert the invasion of Japan's mainland and minimize American casualties, thus contributing to an early conclusion of the war."*

American politicians have continued to espouse this view. Primary among them was Harry S. Truman, the one-term president responsible for making the decision to drop the bombs in August of 1945. In his 1955 memoirs, Truman claimed the bombs saved half a million American lives. Truman insisted he felt no remorse and bragged that *"he never lost any sleep over that decision,"* while simultaneously referring to the Japanese as *"savages, ruthless, merciless, and fanatic."* By 1991, George H.W. Bush claimed dropping the bombs saved millions of American lives. Historian Peter Kuznick sums up the ever-increasing number of American lives saved due to these actions:

> *"...from the War Department's 1945 prediction of 46,000 dead to Truman's 1955 insistence that General George Marshall feared losing a half million American lives to Stimson's 1947 claim of over 1,000,000 casualties to George H.W. Bush's 1991 defense of Truman's 'tough calculating decision, [which] spared millions of American lives,'[11] to the 1995 estimate of a crew member on Bock's Car, the plane that bombed Nagasaki, who asserted that the bombing saved six million lives—one million Americans and five million Japanese."*

Twenty years ago (the 50th anniversary of the bombings) when the Smithsonian Museum tried to create a thought-provoking display about *Enola Gay* (the plane that dropped the first bomb on Hiroshima), the Senate threw a temper tantrum and passed a resolution condemning the move. The resolution stated that

"...the Enola Gay during World War II was momentous in helping to bring World War II to a merciful end, which resulted in saving the lives of Americans and Japanese."

Of course, none of these figures about saved American lives are true. When President Truman was contemplating dropping the bomb, he consulted a panel of experts on the number of American soldiers that would be killed if the U.S. launched an invasion of the two main Japanese islands. According to historian Christian Appy,

*"[Truman] did...ask a panel of military experts to offer an estimate of how many Americans might be killed if the United States launched the two major invasions of the Japanese home islands...Their figure: **40,000—far below the half-million he would cite after the war.** "[emphasis added]*

Americans are socialized to believe that dropping the bombs was necessary to end the war. As recently as January 2015, a Pew poll found that 56% of Americans believed dropping the two atomic devices was justified. Only 34% said it was not justified. This American attitude is understandable given the downplaying of Japanese deaths and the exaggeration of American lives saved in high school history books.

In spite of this public perception, dropping the nuclear bombs was totally unnecessary from a military standpoint. America's leading generals voiced their concerns before and after the bombs were dropped. General Eisenhower, Supreme Commander of the Allied Forces in Western Europe, reacted to the news in a way that contradicts politicians' narratives:

*"During his [Secretary of War Henry L. Stimson] recitation of the relevant facts, I had been conscious of a feeling of depression and so I voiced to him my grave misgivings, first on the basis of my belief that Japan was **already defeated** and that dropping the bomb was completely unnecessary, and secondly because I thought that our country should avoid shocking world opinion by the use of a weapon whose employment was, I thought, **no longer mandatory as a measure to save American lives,"** he said. [emphasis added]*

General Douglas MacArthur, Supreme Commander of Allied Forces in the Pacific, was not even consulted about the use of the bomb. He was only notified two days before the first bomb was dropped. When he was informed he thought *"'…it was completely unnecessary from a military point of view.' MacArthur said that the war might 'end sooner than some think.' The Japanese were 'already beaten.'"*

Tough, cigar-smoking "hawk," General Curtis LeMay—who was responsible for the firebombing of Japanese cities—was also disappointed with the decision to drop the bomb. In an exchange with reporters he said,

> *"The war would have been over in two weeks without the Russians entering **and without the atomic bomb**. [emphasis added]"*
>
> *"You mean that, sir? Without the Russians and the atomic bomb?" one journalist asked.*
>
> *"The atomic bomb had nothing to do with the end of the war at all," LeMay replied.*

Admiral Chester Nimitz, Commander in Chief of the Pacific Fleet, sent out the following public statement: *"**The atomic bomb played no decisive part**, from a purely military standpoint, in the defeat of Japan."* [emphasis added]

While Eisenhower, MacArthur, LeMay, and Nimitz believed the dropping of the bombs to be unnecessary, Chief of Staff Admiral William D. Leahy went even further, insisting that even the contemplated invasion of Japan was unnecessary to end the war. He said,

> *"I was unable to see any justification…**for an invasion of an already thoroughly defeated Japan.** My conclusion, with which the naval representatives agreed, was that America's least expensive course of action was to continue to intensify the air and sea blockade…I believe that a completely blockaded Japan would then fall by its own weight." [emphasis added]*

At the conclusion of the war in the Pacific, President Truman appointed a panel of 1000 experts to study the conflict. One third of the experts were civilians and two-thirds were military. The panel issued its report, entitled "United States Strategic Bombing Survey"—a 108 volume publication on the Pacific front. The survey makes the following damning conclusion about the necessity of dropping the atomic bombs and invading Japan:

> *"Nevertheless, it seems clear that, even without the atomic bombing attacks, air supremacy over Japan could have exerted sufficient pressure to bring about **unconditional surrender and obviate the need for invasion.** Based on a detailed investigation of all the facts, and supported by the testimony of the surviving Japanese leaders involved, it is the Survey's opinion that certainly prior to 31 December 1945,...**Japan would have surrendered even if the atomic bombs had not been dropped, even if Russia had not entered the war, and even if no invasion had been planned or contemplated.**" [emphasis added]*

Even the Japanese leaders knew they were defeated. They were even secretly willing to negotiate an unconditional surrender. According to the survey, there was

> *"...a plan to send Prince Konoye to Moscow as a special emissary with instructions from the cabinet to negotiate for peace on terms less than unconditional surrender, but with private instructions from the Emperor to secure peace at any price."*

If dropping the bombs was not necessary, and if Japan was even willing to contemplate an unconditional surrender, then why were the bombs dropped at all? One reason referenced by several historians was to project American power against the future enemy in the Cold War, the U.S.S.R. As the *Christian Science Monitor* noted in 1992,

> *"Gregg Herken...observes...that 'responsible traditional as well as revisionist accounts of the decision to drop the bomb now recognize that the act had behind...a possible diplomatic advantage concerning Russia.' Yale Prof. Gaddis Smith writes: 'It has been demonstrated that the **decision to bomb Japan was centrally connected to Truman's confrontational approach to the Soviet Union.**'"[emphasis added]*

THE DECISION TO DROP THE BOMB

America had the bomb. Now what?

When Harry Truman learned of the success of the Manhattan Project, he knew he was faced with a decision of unprecedented gravity. The capacity to end the war with Japan was in his hands, but it would involve unleashing the most terrible weapon ever known.

American soldiers and civilians were weary from four years of war, yet the Japanese military was refusing to give up their fight. American forces occupied Okinawa and Iwo Jima and were intensely fire bombing Japanese cities. But Japan had an army of 2 million strong stationed in the home islands.

For Truman, the choice whether or not to use the atomic bomb was the most difficult decision of his life.

First, an Allied demand for an immediate unconditional surrender was made to the leadership in Japan. Although the demand stated that refusal would result in total destruction, no mention of any new weapons of mass destruction was made. The Japanese military command rejected the request for unconditional surrender, but there were indications that a conditional surrender was possible.

Regardless, on August 6, 1945, a plane called the *Enola Gay* dropped an atomic bomb on the city of Hiroshima. Instantly, 70,000 Japanese citizens were vaporized. In the months and years that followed, an additional 100,000 perished from burns and radiation sickness.

Two days later, the Soviet Union declared war on Japan. On August 9, a second atomic bomb was dropped on Nagasaki, where 80,000 Japanese people perished.

On August 14, 1945, the Japanese surrendered.

Critics have charged that Truman's decision was a barbaric act that brought negative long-term consequences to the United States. A new age of nuclear terror led to a dangerous arms race.

Some military analysts insist that Japan was on its knees and the bombings were simply unnecessary. The American government was accused of racism on the grounds that such a device would never have been used against white civilians.

The ethical debate over the decision to drop the atomic bomb will never be resolved. The bombs did, however, bring an end to the most destructive war in history. The Manhattan Project that produced it demonstrated the possibility of how a nation's resources could be mobilized.

Pandora's box was now open. The question that came flying out was, "How will the world use its nuclear capability?" It is a question still being addressed on a daily basis.

— "The Decision to Drop the Bomb," US History.org, http://www.ushistory.org/us/51g.asp. Licensed Under CC BY 4.0 International.

Secondly, there was a rather large incentive to use the bomb—to test its effectiveness. On that subject, the most succinct quote comes from Admiral William F. Halsey, Jr., Commander U.S. Third Fleet. He said, "*[The scientists] had this toy and they wanted to try it out, so they dropped it. . . . It killed a lot of Japs, but the Japs had put out a lot of peace feelers through Russia long before.*"

According to the Center for Strategic and International Studies, the Manhattan Project (the project to build the bomb) cost the U.S. an estimated $1,889,604,000 (in 1945 dollars) through December 31, 1945. That comes out to $25,051,739,964.00 in today's dollars. The Center goes on to add:

"Weapons were created to be used. By 1945, the bombing of civilians was already an established practice. In fact, the earlier U.S. firebombing campaign of Japan, which began in 1944, killed an estimated 315,922 Japanese, a greater number than the estimated deaths attributed to the atomic bombing of Hiroshima and Nagasaki."

From a purely numbers perspective, the detonation of the atomic bombs killed fewer people than the firebombing of the 67 Japanese cities with napalm. The sick logic of war is this: having killed close to 316,000 Japanese people by firebombing cities, killing 100,000–200,000 more is just as justifiable.

It is clear from the recitation of some of the evidence that the dropping of the atomic bombs was not necessary to end the war.

It was not necessary to obviate the U.S. invasion of Japan (which in and of itself was not necessary) and it was not necessary for an unconditional surrender.

It is time for the United States to stop believing that the infamous nuclear attacks were justified. On that front, there is some hope. Back in 1991, 63% of Americans believed dropping the bombs was justified, compared to 56% today. Clearly, the numbers are heading in the right direction.

The U.S. government could easily nudge public opinion in the appropriate direction by issuing a public apology for the dropping of these weapons of mass destruction on the cities of Hiroshima and Nagasaki. The U.S. is capable of doing this. In 1988, the U.S. Senate voted to compensate Japanese Americans for interning them during WWII. In 1993, President Bill Clinton signed a formal letter of apology. The U.S. did the right thing by apologizing to Japanese Americans. It is time to extend this apology to the entire Japanese nation.

Nuclear Nonproliferation: A No-Nonsense International Need

George Bunn

No expert is worthier of expressing an opinion on the Nuclear Nonproliferation Treaty of 1968 than the author of the following viewpoint. George Bunn was the first general counsel for the US Arms Control and Disarmament Agency, which helped negotiate the treaty. He also later became US ambassador to the Geneva Disarmament Conference. Bunn dissects the events of nearly a half-century ago with hindsight and states that the nations of the world must remain vigilant in their work and their desire to prevent any nuclear exchange. He cites a shifting international landscape but claims also that the fundamental desire of world leaders and their citizens to avoid a catastrophe must never weaken.

Fifty years ago this month, President Dwight D. Eisenhower gave his "Atoms for Peace" address to the UN General Assembly. He proposed to share nuclear materials and information for peaceful purposes with other countries through a new international agency. That speech led to negotiations which, several years later, created the International Atomic Energy Agency (IAEA). The IAEA today has the dual responsibility of helping countries that do not have nuclear weapons to engage in peaceful nuclear programs while ensuring that they do not make nuclear weapons. In the nuclear Nonproliferation Treaty (NPT) of 1968, the IAEA gained authority

"The Nuclear Nonproliferation Treaty: History and Current Problems," by George Bunn, Arms Control Association. Reprinted with Permission from Arms Control Today/Arms Control Association.

for policing the nuclear activities of member countries to ensure that those without nuclear weapons did not acquire them.

Today, the NPT is a worldwide treaty that bans all members except the United Kingdom, China, France, Russia, and the United States from having nuclear weapons and commits those five states to eventually eliminating their atomic arsenals. The treaty provides the norm and the foundation for an international regime to prevent the spread of nuclear weapons around the world. The 187 states that subscribe to the NPT include all significant states of concern with the exception of India, Israel, Pakistan, and—arguably—North Korea.[1] According to Ambassador Robert T. Grey, a former U.S. arms control negotiator, the NPT is "in many ways an agreement as important as the UN Charter itself."[2] Yet, many believe that the NPT regime is battered and in need of strengthening.[3]

The NPT has in fact suffered major blows. Since 1991, uranium enrichment, plutonium separation, and other possibly weapons-related activities that Iraq, North Korea, and Iran hid from IAEA inspectors have been discovered. Iraq's weapons program was found after the 1991 Persian Gulf War thanks to UN Security Council orders demanding more intrusive inspections than were then required by IAEA inspection standards. North Korea's weapons program later became known through intelligence, IAEA inspections, and North Korea's own admissions. The IAEA's discovery of Iran's failure to disclose experiments with plutonium separation and uranium enrichment to inspectors has recently led to a standoff with Tehran.

Historically, the IAEA has rarely demanded inspections beyond the perimeter of reactors or related nuclear sites that had been declared open for inspection by the countries where they were located. Further, uranium enrichment and plutonium separation does not violate the NPT if done for peaceful purposes under IAEA inspection. In fact, a number of more developed countries (e.g., Japan) conduct such activities. In the three countries where uranium enrichment or plutonium separation was thought to have been conducted for weapons purposes—Iran, Iraq, and North Korea—the activities had taken place largely at locations not declared open for inspection to the IAEA.

Moreover, that North Korea and Iran both obtained enrichment technology from Pakistan suggests dangers to the NPT regime from nonparties that are not bound by the treaty's prohibition against assisting non-nuclear-weapon states in acquiring nuclear weapons. The back-to-back nuclear tests by New Delhi and Islamabad in 1998 illustrate the dangers that an arms race in South Asia can have and suggest the temptation that such tests could encourage current non-nuclear-weapon parties to withdraw from the treaty in order to follow suit.

At the same time, the United States has not complied with some of its own NPT-created obligations. For example, in 1995 the United States won the agreement of the non-nuclear-weapon NPT states-parties to extend the NPT indefinitely by promising to negotiate a Comprehensive Test Ban Treaty (CTBT). The treaty was duly negotiated and signed by President Bill Clinton in 1996, but the Senate failed to ratify it in 1999. The Bush administration now opposes the CTBT, and the Senate is unlikely to consider it again, at least before the next election. That reflects a broader tendency by this Bush administration to downgrade treaties and regimes and to upgrade unilateral efforts, such as the pre-emptive use of force against Iraq, to enforce compliance with nonproliferation.

In addition, the Bush administration has undertaken efforts to create new types of nuclear weapons that might well require new testing.[4] Thus, while pushing other countries to reject the acquisition of nuclear weapons for their defense, the United States seems to be relying ever more heavily on nuclear weapons for its own defense. This double standard constitutes another threat to the NPT regime.

These points are all relevant to the status of the NPT today and will be explained in more detail below or in other articles in this issue.

Early Nonproliferation Efforts

Eisenhower's 1953 "Atoms for Peace" speech came after the failure of earlier U.S. nonproliferation efforts. At the end of World War II, when the United States had the only nuclear weapons in the world, President Harry Truman proposed to destroy the U.S. nuclear arsenal if other countries would agree not to acquire nuclear weapons and would permit inspections to verify that agreement. The "Baruch Plan" of the Truman administration would have given an agency under the jurisdiction of the UN Security Council a monopoly over research on how to make nuclear explosives and the power, free of veto and backed up by military force if necessary, to conduct inspections in other countries to make sure they were not making nuclear weapons. The United States, however, would not surrender its weapons to the agency until inspectors were on duty in the Soviet Union and in other countries with nuclear potential. The Soviet Union rejected this approach; it was already seeking its own nuclear weapons. Skeptical about the Baruch Plan being debated at the United Nations, the U.S. Congress enacted the 1946 Atomic Energy Act with provisions designed to keep nuclear technology secret from other countries.[5]

By contrast, Eisenhower proposed providing assistance to other countries in the peaceful uses of atomic energy. As a result of his proposal, the U.S. Atomic Energy Act was amended to authorize nuclear assistance to others, and the IAEA was created to provide both assistance and inspectors for peaceful nuclear activities. The United States, followed by the Soviet Union, France, and others, began providing research reactors that used weapons-usable, highly enriched uranium (though usually in lesser amounts than needed for a weapon) to non-nuclear-weapon states around the world. These transfers and the training that accompanied the reactors helped scientists in many countries learn about nuclear fission and its potential uses.

As these scientists moved up the nuclear learning curve, global support increased for controlling the spread of the new technology in order to prevent its use for weapons. Soon, debate about nonproliferation in the UN General Assembly produced a 1961 consensus Irish resolution saying that countries already having nuclear weapons would "undertake to refrain from relinquishing control" of them to others and would refrain "from transmitting information for their manufacture to States not possessing" them. Countries without nuclear weapons would agree not to receive or manufacture them. These ideas were the basis for the NPT.[6]

The United States submitted a simple draft treaty based on this resolution to the Soviet Union when a new 18-nation Disarmament Conference opened in Geneva in 1962. The Soviet response was to insist on a treaty that would prohibit the arrangements that the United States then had with NATO allies such as West Germany for deployment, in their countries, of U.S. nuclear weapons under the control of U.S. soldiers—weapons to be used to protect these countries, if necessary, in the event of an attack on them by the Soviet Union and its allies. The Soviet proposal and U.S. plans for a "multilateral force" of naval vessels with nuclear weapons— vessels manned by sailors from participating NATO countries and under NATO command—became major obstacles to agreement. By then, the multilateral force plan was strongly supported only by West Germany. However, for the United States to agree that an NPT should prohibit U.S. allies not having nuclear weapons from joining in control of U.S. nuclear weapons in peacetime required meetings with President Lyndon Johnson at Camp David, further negotiations with Soviet representatives, recommendations to the president from an important committee of distinguished advisers, lengthy discussions with West Germany and other allies, a congressional resolution urging negotiation of a nonproliferation treaty, and bureaucratic maneuvering to gain Johnson's approval for proposed treaty language.

In the compromise, the United States gave up on the multilateral force; the Soviets gave up on a prohibition against U.S. deployment of nuclear weapons in West Germany (and other allied countries), provided the weapons remained under sole control of U.S. personnel. The non-nuclear-weapon states were asked to accept draft language which prohibited them from having nuclear weapons and which called for the IAEA to be permitted to carry out inspections to guarantee that their nuclear programs were limited to peaceful uses. In addition, the United Kingdom, the Soviet Union, and the United States agreed to provide assistance to non-nuclear-weapon NPT members in their pursuit of peaceful uses of nuclear energy and agreed to conduct future negotiations to halt the nuclear arms race and reduce their nuclear weapons with the goal of achieving nuclear disarmament.

Negotiations then began for gaining acceptance of these provisions by important non-nuclear-weapon governments and their parliaments and for prescribing the inspections that would be conducted by the IAEA pursuant to the NPT. India, which had participated actively in the NPT negotiations as a country without nuclear weapons, refused to join. It wanted to retain the option to produce its own nuclear weapons as its then-adversary, China, already had. Pakistan, another adversary of India, refused to join because India would not. Israel, which the United States had tried to restrain from acquiring nuclear weapons in separate negotiations during the 1960s, also refused to join. China and France had not participated in the NPT negotiations but had acquired nuclear weapons before its negotiation was completed. The NPT draft permitted them to join the treaty with the same rights and duties as the other nuclear-weapon states—the United Kingdom, the Soviet Union, and the United States. They did so later.

States began signing the treaty in 1968, and it went into force in 1970. However, the negotiations at the IAEA among parties and potential parties on the scope of inspections for non-nuclear-weapon parties continued for several years. Many countries, including West European allies of the United States, did not ratify the treaty until these negotiations were completed to their satisfaction.[7] There were also further negotiations every five years at NPT review conferences. These dealt with implementation of treaty provisions such as those promising assistance to non-nuclear-weapon states for peaceful uses and calling for reductions of nuclear weapons and for nuclear disarmament. At an important conference in 1995, the treaty was extended indefinitely from its initial 25-year term. [8] The 1995 decision and the review conference of 2000 focused particular attention on the NPT-related promises of the nuclear-weapon states to "cease the nuclear arms race" including stopping nuclear testing, negotiating reductions of nuclear weapons, and eventually achieving nuclear disarmament.[9]

Current Problems

Even as the legal regime was expanded by these agreements, the NPT came under strain elsewhere. One of the most significant blows was Iraq's demonstrated ability to hide its nuclear-weapon-making efforts from IAEA inspectors before the Gulf War. With inspection authority from UN Security Council resolutions adopted after that war—authority beyond what the 1970s negotiations on NPT verification standards had given the IAEA—inspectors found previously hidden Iraqi efforts to enrich uranium to make nuclear weapons and even an attempt to use (for a weapon) highly enriched research-reactor uranium provided for peaceful purposes by France and the Soviet Union.[10]

These findings produced a major effort to strengthen the IAEA's NPT inspection authority through an additional protocol. The IAEA parties who negotiated the 1997 model for this protocol did not agree, however, that the NPT required its parties to accept the model, as had been the case with earlier IAEA safeguards standards. It is now up to each NPT party to negotiate with the IAEA a revised safeguards agreement pursuant to the model.[11] As of mid-2003, only 81 of 187 NPT states had negotiated new safeguards agreements; only 37, or about 20 percent, had given final approval to them through parliamentary or other ratification. [12] Even the United States has not yet adopted legislation to implement its new safeguards agreement. Some non-nuclear-weapon states may be holding back, asking why they should take on more nonproliferation obligations when, as they perceive it, the United States rejects an important one—the CTBT prohibition on nuclear testing—and then proposes new types of nuclear weapons for itself.[13]

After the experience with Iraq, IAEA inspectors sought new techniques to deal with other problem states such as North Korea. Some evidence was produced by IAEA inspectors in the 1990s using a new technique called "environmental monitoring"— testing for small traces of evidence of nuclear activities in the air, on walls or vegetation in areas within or surrounding a nuclear site, or in streams or rivers nearby. This is explicitly authorized in the 1997 Mode Additional Protocol for use even at sites far from the reactors that a country has declared open for inspection.[14] Results from using these and other techniques at declared sites encouraged the IAEA to press North Korea for broader inspections in the early 1990s, but Pyongyang refused. A stalemate between North Korea and the IAEA eventually led to bilateral negotiations between the United States and North Korea and the 1994 Agreed Framework between the two countries which called for Pyongyang to dismantle a reactor whose spent fuel rods had apparently been used by North Korea to produce plutonium. Pyongyang was also asked to provide information about its past activities. These steps were to be in exchange for the construction of new, more proliferation-resistant nuclear reactors from South Korea and Japan, as well as interim supplies of heavy-fuel oil from the United States.[15] However, North Korea appears to have engaged in nuclear-weapon activities at other sites after the 1994 agreement was inked. During 2002-2003, North Korea and the United States each concluded that the 1994 agreement was not to their liking, and North Korea announced its withdrawal from the NPT.[16]

Discovery of Iran's failure to disclose experiments with plutonium separation and uranium enrichment to IAEA inspectors has triggered concern since last year. Using environmental monitoring and other techniques at declared sites and undeclared sites that Iran permitted them to check, the IAEA inspectors uncovered many suspicious items, including tiny samples of enriched uranium, tubes apparently used for enriching uranium in centrifuges, and stocks of unenriched uranium—none of which Iran had reported to the IAEA. In negotiations with the United Kingdom, France, and Germany, Iran agreed to sign an additional protocol authorizing broader inspections in Iran and to put aside its uranium-enrichment plans, at least for the time being. Though the IAEA director-general's report shows that Iran had not disclosed to earlier inspectors its uranium-enrichment efforts or an experiment in plutonium separation, he concluded that the IAEA lacked direct proof that these efforts were for the purpose of making weapons—to the consternation of officials in the United States. The IAEA Board of Governors then adopted, with U.S. support, a decision to order continued inspections in Iran for clandestine activities.[17]

The uranium-enrichment and plutonium-separation efforts of Iraq, North Korea, and Iran have produced renewed calls for the NPT not to permit such efforts even if subject to IAEA inspection. The concern is that, once a country gains access to this technology, it might then withdraw from the NPT (as North Korea did) and use its stocks of weapons-usable uranium or plutonium to make weapons. The Nuclear Supplier's Group (NSG) had earlier recommended that new uranium-enrichment and plutonium-separation plants of non-nuclear-weapon states be placed under multilateral ownership and control so that the co-owners from the different countries could check on each other.[18] However, Japan; some western European non-nuclear-weapon countries; and Argentina, Brazil, South Africa, and a few others, as well as all the nuclear-weapon states, have or have experimented with enrichment or reprocessing facilities. Should these all now be subject to a rule requiring multilateral ownership and oversight? Would limiting the requirement to non-nuclear-weapon countries be regarded as adding further insult to the NPT's existing discrimination in favor of nuclear-weapon states? IAEA Director-General Mohamed ElBaradei has recommended that all enrichment and reprocessing facilities used for civilian purposes should be multilaterally owned and controlled in the future, with each country involved being urged to check on what its partner countries are doing to make sure that the enriched uranium or separated plutonium is not used for weapons purposes.[19]

The Bush administration has pressed hard on Iraq, Iran, and North Korea to restrain them from acquiring nuclear weapons, but it has done so sometimes in unilateral or domineering ways that seem inconsistent with a multilateral regime like that of the NPT. The American-led, counter-proliferation-justified, preventive-war invasion of Iraq in 2003 that the United States waged without UN Security Council authorization is a recent example. At the time, the invasion was said to be necessary to prevent Iraq from again acquiring nuclear, biological, or chemical weapons or long-range missiles. It took place even though Security Council-authorized inspections, consistent with the NPT, were going on in Iraq to look for these weapons. It resulted in UN inspectors being withdrawn from Iraq for their own safety. U.S inspectors have subsequently found little evidence of ongoing biological, chemical, or nuclear weapons programs but the decision reflected Bush's tendency to downgrade treaties and international efforts in favor of more proactive proliferation efforts."[20]

Likewise, the Senate failed to ratify the CTBT in 1999. The Bush administration has not asked the Senate to reconsider that vote and instead has said that the United States "will not become a party" to that treaty.[21] At the same time, the administration seeks money from Congress for new types of nuclear weapons—ones that may well need testing before the United States would rely on them. However, in 1995, when the United States negotiated an agreement with all the non-nuclear-weapon states to extend the NPT beyond 1995, it agreed to negotiate a CTBT by 1996 as part of the price it had to pay to gain agreement to renew the NPT.[22] The CTBT was negotiated by 1996. Then, in the 2000 NPT review conference, the Clinton administration agreed on "the importance and urgency" of ratification of the CTBT "without delay" to "achieve the early entry into force" of the treaty even though the Senate then had no plans to vote again on the CTBT.[23] Is the CTBT such an essential element of the nonproliferation regime that U.S. failure to join it could provide persuasive justification for withdrawal from the NPT for those who choose to do so?[24]

Other problems of this sort occurred with Article VI of the NPT, agreed to in the original treaty negotiations in order to gain the support for the treaty of non-nuclear-weapon states. In that provision, the United States and the other recognized nuclear-weapon states promised to negotiate nuclear-weapon reductions with the goal of nuclear disarmament. Then, to gain the votes of these parties for extension of the NPT in 1995, the United States agreed to pursue "progressive efforts to reduce nuclear weapons globally, with the ultimate goal of eliminating those weapons."[25] At the 2000 NPT review conference, the Clinton administration made similar commitments. It also promised to implement START II (negotiated in the prior Bush administration) and to conclude "START III [more reductions] as soon as possible while preserving and strengthening the [Anti-Ballistic Missile (ABM)] Treaty as the cornerstone of strategic stability."[26]

These promises were shredded when the present Bush administration withdrew from the ABM Treaty. The withdrawal nullified START II because the Russian Duma had conditioned its approval vote for START II on a continuation of the ABM Treaty. The substitute for START II negotiated with Russia by President George W. Bush, the Strategic Offensive Reductions Treaty of 2002, required withdrawal of warheads from many long-range missiles on each side to the end that, by 2012, no more than 2,200 warheads would be deployed on either side.[27] The treaty, however, does not require the warheads to be destroyed, calls for no inspections, has a more permissive withdrawal clause than in START II, and contains no stated plan for a subsequent treaty such as START III that would require further reductions. Does this satisfy the NPT commitment to negotiate toward nuclear disarmament? ElBaradei has suggested that the United States may be employing a double standard by not actually cutting its own arsenal of nuclear weapons (as distinct from its missiles)

How Many Nukes Would It Take to Render Earth Uninhabitable?

Currently, there are over 15,000 nuclear weapons in the world. Out of 196 countries, only nine possess nuclear weapons. And more than 90% of the world's nukes are owned by just two countries: the United States and Russia.

But did you know that even a minor nuclear conflict—one that uses only a fraction of the nuclear weapons currently in existence—could wreak havoc on the global climate and affect billions of people across the world?

A 2014 report published in the journal *Earth's Future* found that even a regional war of 100 nuclear detonations would produce 5 teragrams of black soot (that's 5,000,000,000 kg!) that would rise up to Earth's stratosphere and block sunlight. This would produce a sudden drop in global temperatures that could last longer than 25 years and temporarily destroy much of the Earth's protective ozone layer. This could also cause as much as an 80% increase in UV radiation on Earth's surface and destroy both land and sea-based ecosystems, potentially leading to global nuclear famine.

Michael Mills, an atmospheric scientist at the National Center for Atmospheric Research in Boulder, Colorado and the study's lead author, summarized it best:

In the 1980s, we learned that global thermonuclear war could render the planet close to uninhabitable. Now, we know that even [regional] nuclear war can cause great suffering worldwide, with potential for a lot of people to die from starvation in regions very far from a conflict.

Seems like now might be a good time to start dismantling some of those 15,000 nuclear weapons.

The good news is: We don't have to sit idly by and watch our fate unfold before us. We can do something about this. The problem of existing nuclear weapons isn't scientific or technological—it's political. There are only nine countries in the world that actually have nuclear weapons; to achieve global zero, we only need to influence a small (though powerful) group of global leaders. Let's take a stand and demand action from those leaders to eliminate nuclear weapons once and for all.

This is one of the most urgent human rights issues of our time.

— "How many nukes would it take to render Earth uninhabitable?" by Ryan Rastegar, Global Zero, July 9, 2015.

while attempting to restrain other countries from acquiring nuclear weapons.[28]

To gain the agreement of the non-nuclear-weapon NPT parties to the treaty's extension in 1995, the United States also made promises in connection with a UN Security Council resolution calling for what are called negative security assurances, which for the United States was a promise not to use nuclear weapons against non-nuclear-weapon NPT parties unless they attack the United States while in alliance with another nuclear-weapon state.[29] Yet, in its Nuclear Posture Review of 2001 and its National Strategy on Weapons of Mass Destruction of 2002, the Bush administration made clear that it was prepared to use nuclear weapons against a non-nuclear-weapon NPT party that threatened the use of chemical or biological weapons against the United States or its allies whether or not this NPT party was allied with a nuclear-weapon state.[30] Thus, the United States watered down another promise that was important to gaining the support of non-nuclear-weapon NPT states-parties for renewal of the NPT in 1995. Whether all these problems will produce further withdrawals from the NPT is, of course, unknown, but they might be used as excuses for withdrawal by any who want to do so.

What Has the NPT Accomplished?

The NPT nonproliferation norm, the long-term efforts of the United States and others to gain acceptance of it, and the international inspections the NPT produced deserve significant credit for the fact that the world does not now have 30 or more countries with nuclear weapons.

In 1963 the Department of Defense looked at the motivations of the "nuclear-capable" countries at the time and estimated for Kennedy that perhaps 10 more of them could have nuclear weapons and suitable delivery vehicles in less than a decade if nothing was done to prevent such a scenario from unfolding; they were the remaining major industrialized Group of Seven allies of the United States plus China, Czechoslovakia, India, Israel, Poland, and Sweden.[31] Thus, based on the 1963 list, 14 or more countries could have had nuclear weapons by the early 1970s.

The Defense Department's list did not include Switzerland, Australia, South Korea, or Taiwan, which all had scientists who were then considering or would soon consider how to build nuclear weapons. It did not include South Africa, which later built several nuclear weapons, then gave them up and, like the others, joined the NPT. It did not include any republics of the Soviet Union. Three republics—Belarus, Kazakhstan, and Ukraine—had Soviet weapons on their territory when the Soviet Union collapsed and gave them up to join the NPT after negotiations with Russia and the United States supplied them with financial incentives and promises not to attack them with nuclear weapons. Without the NPT norm, these countries would probably not have given their inherited weapons up. The Pentagon list did not include Argentina and Brazil, which later began nuclear weapons programs but then negotiated a bilateral agreement not to acquire nuclear weapons and joined the NPT—turning rivalry into cooperation in response to the norm of the NPT and of a Latin American Nuclear-Weapon-Free Zone agreement.[32]

North Korea, Pakistan, Iran, and Iraq began later and were not on the Pentagon's 1963 list either.[33] If there had been no NPT, if all these countries plus the ones on the list acquired nuclear weapons, the total would have been at least 28 by now. Some neighbors and rivals would then probably have been motivated to acquire nuclear weapons themselves. What would the total have become? More than 30 countries with nuclear weapons? Today, we have nine counting North Korea but not Iran.

The single most important factor in producing this success has been the nonproliferation norm established by the NPT and the incentives for remaining non-nuclear that the NPT helped initiate. The next most important factor has probably been leadership, cooperative efforts, and financial assistance in some cases from the United States working with many other NPT parties.[34] Given the more difficult nonproliferation and security challenges of today, it is vital that U.S. leadership be used to strengthen, not to weaken or abandon, the nuclear nonproliferation regime.

Notes

1. Some believe that North Korea's withdrawal was invalid and count it still as a party to the treaty.

2. See Bipartisan Security Group, *Status of Nuclear Non-Proliferation Treaty, Interim Report* (*Global Security Institute,* June 2003), preface.

3. See Mohamed ElBaradei, "Towards a Safer World," *The Economist* (October 18, 2003), pp. 47-48; Ariel Levite, "Never Say Never Again," *International Security* (Winter 2002–2003), p. 59; T. Ogilvie-White and John Simpson, "The NPT and Its 2003 Prep Com Session: A Regime in Need of Intensive Care," *The Nonproliferation Review* (Spring 2003), p. 40; Stanley Foundation Conference, "Global Disarmament Regimes: A Future or a Failure?" (2003), p. 2; "Nuclear Breakout," *The New York Times* (July 27, 2003), p. 12.

4. See Sidney Drell et al., "A Strategic Choice: New Bunker Busters vs. Nonproliferation," *Arms Control Today* (March 2003), p. 3.

5. George Bunn, *Arms Control by Committee: Managing Negotiations with the Russians* (Stanford University Press, 1992), pp. 59–72.

6. Leonard Weiss, "Atoms for Peace," *Bulletin of the Atomic Scientists* (November-December 2003), pp. 34, 37, 41; Bunn, *Arms Control by Committee,* pp. 64–66. Arms Control by Committee provides a more detailed account of the history of the NPT's negotiation.

7. Glenn T. Seaborg with Benjamin S. Loeb, *Stemming the Tide: Arms Control in the Johnson Years* (Lexington Books, 1987), p. 305; Charles N. Van Doren, "Some Perspectives on Supplier Control," in *The Nuclear Suppliers and Nonproliferation,* eds. Rodney Jones et al. (Lexington Books, 1985), p. 17.

8. "Decision: Extension of the Treaty on Non-Proliferation of Nuclear Weapons," May 1, 1995, NPT/CONF.1995/32/DEC.3.

9. *Ibid.*; "2000 Review Conference of the Parties to the Treaty on the Non-Proliferation of Nuclear Weapons, Final Document," 2000 NPT/CONF.2000/28 (May 22, 2000). See Bipartisan Security Group, *Status of Nuclear Non-Proliferation Treaty,* pp. 2, 11–16.

10. See Joseph Cirincione, John Wolfsthal, and Miriam Rajkumar, *Deadly Arsenals: Tracking Weapons of Mass Destruction* (Carnegie Endowment for International Peace, 2002), pp. 271, 273–275; George Bunn and Chaim Braun, "Terrorism Potential of Research Reactors Compared with Power Reactors," *American Behavioral Sciences* (February 2003), pp. 714, 717–718.

11. See "Strengthening the Effectiveness and Improving the Efficiency of the Safeguards System," IAEA GC(40)17 (August 23, 1996), Annex I. For a view that authority for the requirements of the protocol could have been interpreted to be obligatory rather than voluntary, see George Bunn, "Inspection for Clandestine Nuclear Activities: Does the Nuclear Non-Proliferation Treaty Provide Legal Authority for the IAEA's Proposals for Reform?" *Nuclear Law Bulletin* (OECD Nuclear Agency, June 1996), p. 9.

12. See ElBaradei, "Towards a Safer World," pp. 47–48.

13. See Mohamed ElBaradei, "Nuclear Non-Proliferation: Revising the Basics, The Assymmetry Remains," speech at the Carnegie International Non-Proliferation Conference, November 14, 2002; Mohamed ElBaradei, "Curbing Nuclear Proliferation," *Arms Control Today* (November 2003), p. 3.

14. See Bunn, "Inspection for Clandestine Nuclear Activities," pp. 11–12.

15. See Cirincione, Wolstahl and Rajkumar, *Deadly Arsenals*, pp. 241–250; Michael May et al., Verifying the Agreed Framework (Lawrence Livermore National Laboratory, UCRL-ID-142036, 2001), chap. 1.

16. See "Nuclear Weapons on the Korean Peninsula," *Arms Control Today* (May 2003), p. 3.

17. See Brenda Shaffer, "Iran at the Nuclear Threshold," *Arms Control Today* (November 2003), p. 7. The text of the agreement of Iran with the foreign ministers of the United Kingdom, France, and Germany appears at p. 25. For a brief description of the confidential IAEA director-general's report on Iran's nuclear program to the IAEA Board of Governors, see William J. Broad, "Surprise Word on Nuclear Gains by North Korea and Iran," *The New York Times*, November 12, 2003, p. A3.

18. See Carleton Thorne, ed., *A Guide to Nuclear Export Controls* (2001), p. 101 (Nuclear Suppliers' Group Guidelines [Part 1], para. 7); ElBaradei, "Towards a Safer World," pp. 47–48; ElBaradei, "Curbing Nuclear Proliferation."

19. ElBaradei, "Towards a Safer World."

20. Jason D. Ellis, "The Best Defense: Counterproliferation and U.S. National Security," *The Washington Quarterly* 26, no. 2 (Spring 2003), pp. 116–117. For the two national strategy documents most pertinent to U.S. pre-emptive use of force to achieve nonproliferation, see National Strategy of the United States (September 17, 2002), sec. 5; White House, *National Strategy to Combat Weapons of Mass Destruction* (December 11, 2002), sec. V.

21. Sherwood McGinnis, remarks to the UN General Assembly First Committee.

22. See "Principles and Objectives for Nuclear Non-Proliferation and Disarmament," NPT/CONF.1995/32/Dec.2 (May 11, 1995), para. 4(a) (hereinafter "Principles and Objectives").

23. "The 2000 NPT Review Conference, Final Document," NPT/CONF.2000/28, art. VI, para. 5 (hereinafter "2000 NPT Final Document").

24. In the voting on the UN General Assembly First Committee's 2003 resolution supporting the CTBT as important to nonproliferation, the United States was the only country to oppose. See *The First Committee Monitor*, October 27–31, 2003.

25. See "Principles and Objectives," para. 4(b).

26. See "2000 NPT Final Document," art. VI, para. 15, practical step 7.

27. See "Letter of Transmittal and Article-by-Article Analysis of the Treaty on Strategic Offensive Reductions," *Arms Control Today* (July/August 2002).

28. Stephan Pullinger, "U.S. Policy: WMD, Good and Bad," *Disarmament Diplomacy* (October–November 2003), p. 55.

29. George Bunn, "The Legal Status of U.S. Negative Security Assurances to Non-Nuclear Weapon States," *The Nonproliferation Review* (Spring-Summer 1997), p. 1.

30. See *National Strategy to Combat Weapons of Mass Destruction*; U.S. Department of Defense, *Nuclear Posture Review*, (Global Security Institute, December 2002).

31. See Bunn, *Arms Control by Committee*, p. 68.

32. See Mitchell Reiss, B*ridled Ambition: Why Countries Constrain Their Nuclear Capabilities* (Woodrow Wilson Center Press, 1995), chaps. 1–5; Lewis A. Dunn, *Controlling the Bomb: Nuclear Proliferation in the 1980s* (Twentieth Century Fund, 1982), pp. 13–14, 17, 100, 110–111; Thomas Jonter, *Sweden and the Bomb: The Swedish Plans to Acquire Nuclear Weapons, 1945–1972* (Swedish Nuclear Power Inspectorate, 2001), chaps. 4–5.

33. See David Albright and Kevin O'Neill, *Solving the North Korean Nuclear Puzzle (Institute for Science and International Security)*, chap. 1; Reiss, Bridled Ambition, chaps. 1, 5, and 6; Leonard Spector and Jacquiline R. Smith, "North Korea: The Next Nuclear Nightmare?" *Arms Control Today* (March 1991), pp. 8–13.

34. See Levite, "Never Say Never Again," pp. 75–85.

Thirteen Days When the World Cringed

Office of the Historian, US Department of State

The Cold War that resulted in an icy relationship between the United States and Soviet Union thankfully managed to bring the world to the brink of nuclear war only once. And that became known as the Cuban Missile Crisis, which was launched when the latter secretly sought to become nuclear capable in Cuba, where it boasted the potential of placing warheads capable of reaching major American cities. The following viewpoint from the State Department's Office of the Historian takes its readers back to October 1962, when President Kennedy faced down the threat without escalating, using diplomacy, steely resolve, and a naval blockade to end the threat and allow the entire planet to breathe a sigh of relief.

The Cuban Missile Crisis of October 1962 was a direct and dangerous confrontation between the United States and the Soviet Union during the Cold War and was the moment when the two superpowers came closest to nuclear conflict. The crisis was unique in a number of ways, featuring calculations and miscalculations as well as direct and secret communications and miscommunications between the two sides. The dramatic crisis was also characterized by the fact that it was primarily played out at the White House and the Kremlin level with relatively little input from the respective bureaucracies typically involved in the foreign policy process.

"The Cuban Missile Crisis, October 1962," Office of the Historian, US Department of State.

After the failed U.S. attempt to overthrow the Castro regime in Cuba with the Bay of Pigs invasion, and while the Kennedy administration planned Operation Mongoose, in July 1962 Soviet premier Nikita Khrushchev reached a secret agreement with Cuban premier Fidel Castro to place Soviet nuclear missiles in Cuba to deter any future invasion attempt. Construction of several missile sites began in the late summer, but U.S. intelligence discovered evidence of a general Soviet arms build-up on Cuba, including Soviet IL–28 bombers, during routine surveillance flights, and on September 4, 1962, President Kennedy issued a public warning against the introduction of offensive weapons into Cuba. Despite the warning, on October 14 a U.S. U–2 aircraft took several pictures clearly showing sites for medium-range and intermediate-range ballistic nuclear missiles (MRBMs and IRBMs) under construction in Cuba. These images were processed and presented to the White House the next day, thus precipitating the onset of the Cuban Missile Crisis.

Kennedy summoned his closest advisers to consider options and direct a course of action for the United States that would resolve the crisis. Some advisers—including all the Joint Chiefs of Staff—argued for an air strike to destroy the missiles, followed by a U.S. invasion of Cuba; others favored stern warnings to Cuba and the Soviet Union. The President decided upon a middle course. On October 22, he ordered a naval "quarantine" of Cuba. The use of "quarantine" legally distinguished this action from a blockade, which assumed a state of war existed; the use of "quarantine" instead of "blockade" also enabled the United States to receive the support of the Organization of American States.

That same day, Kennedy sent a letter to Khrushchev declaring that the United States would not permit offensive weapons to be delivered to Cuba, and demanded that the Soviets dismantle the missile bases already under construction or completed, and return all offensive weapons to the U.S.S.R. The letter was the first in a series of direct and indirect communications between the White House and the Kremlin throughout the remainder of the crisis.

Cuban Missile Crisis

In October 1962, an American U-2 spy plane secretly photographed nuclear missile sites being built by the Soviet Union on the island of Cuba. President Kennedy did not want the Soviet Union and Cuba to know that he had discovered the missiles. He met in secret with his advisors for several days to discuss the problem.

After many long and difficult meetings, Kennedy decided to place a naval blockade, or a ring of ships, around Cuba. The aim of this "quarantine," as he called it, was to prevent the Soviets from bringing in more military supplies. He demanded the removal of the missiles already there and the destruction of the sites. On October 22, President Kennedy spoke to the nation about the crisis in a televised address.

No one was sure how Soviet leader Nikita Khrushchev would respond to the naval blockade and US demands. But the leaders of both superpowers recognized the devastating possibility of a nuclear war and publicly agreed to a deal in which the Soviets would dismantle the weapon sites in exchange for a pledge from the United States not to invade Cuba. In a separate deal, which remained secret for more than twenty-five years, the United States also agreed to remove its nuclear missiles from Turkey. Although the Soviets removed their missiles from Cuba, they escalated the building of their military arsenal; the missile crisis was over, the arms race was not.

In 1963, there were signs of a lessening of tensions between the Soviet Union and the United States. In his commencement address at American University, President Kennedy urged Americans to reexamine Cold War stereotypes and myths and called for a strategy of peace that would make the world safe for diversity. Two actions also signaled a warming in relations between the superpowers: the establishment of a teletype "Hotline" between the Kremlin and the White House and the signing of the Limited Nuclear Test Ban Treaty on July 25, 1963.

In language very different from his inaugural address, President Kennedy told Americans in June 1963, "For, in the final analysis, our most basic common link is that we all inhabit this small planet. We all breathe the same air. We all cherish our children's future. And we are all mortal."

—"Cuban Missile Crisis," John F. Kennedy Presidential Library and Museum.

The President also went on national television that evening to inform the public of the developments in Cuba, his decision to initiate and enforce a "quarantine," and the potential global consequences if the crisis continued to escalate. The tone of the President's remarks was stern, and the message unmistakable and evocative of the Monroe Doctrine: "It shall be the policy of this nation to regard any nuclear missile launched from Cuba against any nation in the Western Hemisphere as an attack by the Soviet Union on the United States, requiring a full retaliatory response upon the Soviet Union." The Joint Chiefs of Staff announced a military readiness status of DEFCON 3 as U.S. naval forces began implementation of the quarantine and plans accelerated for a military strike on Cuba.

On October 24, Khrushchev responded to Kennedy's message with a statement that the U.S. "blockade" was an "act of aggression" and that Soviet ships bound for Cuba would be ordered to proceed. Nevertheless, during October 24 and 25, some ships turned back from the quarantine line; others were stopped by U.S. naval forces, but they contained no offensive weapons and so were allowed to proceed. Meanwhile, U.S. reconnaissance flights over Cuba indicated the Soviet missile sites were nearing operational readiness. With no apparent end to the crisis in sight, U.S. forces were placed at DEFCON 2—meaning war involving the Strategic Air Command was imminent. On October 26, Kennedy told his advisors it appeared that only a U.S. attack on Cuba would remove the missiles, but he insisted on giving the diplomatic channel a little more time. The crisis had reached a virtual stalemate.

That afternoon, however, the crisis took a dramatic turn. ABC News correspondent John Scali reported to the White House that he had been approached by a Soviet agent suggesting that an agreement could be reached in which the Soviets would remove their missiles from Cuba if the United States promised not to invade the island. While White House staff scrambled to assess the validity of this "back channel" offer, Khrushchev sent Kennedy a message the evening of October 26, which meant it was sent in the middle of the night Moscow time. It was a long, emotional message that raised the specter of nuclear holocaust, and presented a proposed resolution that remarkably resembled what Scali reported earlier that day. "If there is no intention," he said, "to doom the world to the catastrophe of thermonuclear war, then let us not only relax the forces pulling on the ends of the rope, let us take measures to untie that knot. We are ready for this."

Although U.S. experts were convinced the message from Khrushchev was authentic, hope for a resolution was short-lived. The next day, October 27, Khrushchev sent another message indicating that any proposed deal must include the removal of U.S. Jupiter missiles from Turkey. That same day a U.S. U-2 reconnaissance jet was shot down over Cuba. Kennedy and his advisors prepared for an attack on Cuba within days as they searched for any remaining diplomatic resolution. It was determined that Kennedy would ignore the second Khrushchev message and respond to the first one. That night, Kennedy set forth in his message to the Soviet leader proposed steps for the removal of Soviet missiles from Cuba under supervision of the United Nations, and a guarantee that the United States would not attack Cuba.

It was a risky move to ignore the second Khrushchev message. Attorney General Robert Kennedy then met secretly with Soviet Ambassador to the United States, Anatoly Dobrynin, and indicated that the United States was planning to remove the Jupiter missiles from Turkey anyway, and that it would do so soon, but this could not be part of any public resolution of the missile crisis. The next morning, October 28, Khrushchev issued a public statement that Soviet missiles would be dismantled and removed from Cuba.

The crisis was over but the naval quarantine continued until the Soviets agreed to remove their IL–28 bombers from Cuba and, on November 20, 1962, the United States ended its quarantine. U.S. Jupiter missiles were removed from Turkey in April 1963.

The Cuban missile crisis stands as a singular event during the Cold War and strengthened Kennedy's image domestically and internationally. It also may have helped mitigate negative world opinion regarding the failed Bay of Pigs invasion. Two other important results of the crisis came in unique forms. First, despite the flurry of direct and indirect communications between the White House and the Kremlin—perhaps because of it—Kennedy and Khrushchev, and their advisers, struggled throughout the crisis to clearly understand each others' true intentions, while the world hung on the brink of possible nuclear war. In an effort to prevent this from happening again, a direct telephone link between the White House and the Kremlin was established; it became known as the "Hotline." Second, having approached the brink of nuclear conflict, both superpowers began to reconsider the nuclear arms race and took the first steps in agreeing to a nuclear Test Ban Treaty.

We've Been on the Brink of Nuclear War Before

Nick Blackbourn

"Star Wars," the "evil Empire," the Strategic Defense Initiative— the early 1980s under President Reagan was pivotal in the nuclear arms race, with Cold War paranoia at an all-time high. In the following viewpoint by Edinburgh Napier University researcher Nick Blackbourn, two separate incidents from 1983 are used to highlight the tension between the US and the Soviet Union that could've easily led to global nuclear war. Blackbourn cites the book Able Archer 83 *by historian Nate Jones as an invaluable resource on this fraught period in history.*

In the autumn of 1983, at the height of Cold War tensions, the world was only saved from nuclear disaster by the gut feelings of two soldiers during different incidents.

In the first incident, on September 26, a Soviet lieutenant colonel named Stanislav Petrov saw that according to the early-warning system, the Americans had launched numerous missiles against the Russians. He suspected an error and ignored the warnings. His decision to breach protocol and not inform his superiors averted a panicked retaliation.

The second incident is less well known. An American lieutenant general, Leonard Perroots, also chose to ignore warnings—this time that the Soviet Union had gone on high nuclear alert. Like

Petrov, he did nothing, and once again may have prevented an accidental nuclear war.

This was the "Able Archer War Scare," which occurred over ten days in the November of the same year. Recently declassified documents inform *Able Archer 83*, a new book by the Cold War historian Nate Jones which shows just how close the world came to disaster.

Two Tribes

Superpower mutual suspicion was rife in the early 1980s. President Reagan's notorious "Evil Empire" speech, combined with imminent plans to deploy the Pershing II missile system in Europe, which could destroy Moscow with 15 minutes warning, had made the Kremlin especially paranoid. Was the US preparing a first strike to win the Cold War? The USSR's aging and sickly premier, Yuri Andropov, certainly thought Reagan would have no qualms about it. "Reagan is unpredictable. You should expect anything from him," he told Anatoly Dobrynin, Soviet ambassador to the US, at the time.

Another reason the leadership feared a US first strike was Project RYaN, an intricate Soviet intelligence-gathering effort designed to detect preparations for a surprise nuclear attack. It was being kept busy by US aircraft testing Soviet air defence systems by flying towards USSR airspace as part of the PSYOPs (psychological military operations) programme.

The aircraft would deliberately provoke an alert and monitor the Soviet command and control responses, while demonstrating American strength and resolve at the same time. It was an example of the "Peace Through Strength" policy that was seen as vital by Reaganites to help the US emerge from its own perceived era of military weakness under President Carter.

But this US chest-beating led to a resurgence of intense mutual mistrust, with tragic consequences. On September 1 1983, Korean Air Lines flight 007 was shot down by a Russian fighter, killing all 269 passengers and crew. The Kremlin claimed the jet was an American spy plane deep in Russian territory.

In this climate of extreme tension, NATO's "Autumn Forge" war game season kicked off. NATO war games had been an annual occurrence, but the Soviets feared this particular edition might be cover for a surprise attack.

The final phase of the 1983 series, codenamed Able Archer 83, was different from previous years: dummy nuclear weapons, which looked like the real thing, were loaded on to planes. As many as 19,000 American troops were part of a radio-silent airlift to Europe over 170 flights. Military radio networks broadcast references to "nuclear strikes."

This sent Project RYaN into overdrive and the Soviets went on high nuclear alert. Warsaw Pact non-essential military flights were cancelled; nuclear-capable aircraft were placed on alert; nuclear weapons were taken to their launch vehicles; and Chief of the General Staff Nikolai Ogarkov descended into a command bunker outside Moscow to coordinate a possible response to a NATO strike.

There is a debate about the Kremlin's intentions here. Were they genuinely afraid of an attack or simply trying to turn world opinion against the US to prevent Pershing II deployment? At the time, Reagan wondered if the Soviet panic was just "huffing and puffing." In *Able Archer 83*, Nate Jones presents new documentary evidence to suggest the Kremlin's fear was indeed genuine. It was only the decision by Lieutenant General Perroots, sitting in the Able Archer command post, not to respond to this extraordinary alert that avoided further escalation.

The book demonstrates how American leaders failed to appreciate the alarm that their actions might prompt in the Kremlin. In addition, Jones supplies fresh evidence for the argument that Reagan changed his mind on Soviet relations. By his second term, having been influenced by Able Archer and the other events of 1983, he chose to pursue peace far more vigorously than strength.

Why Able Archer Matters

Intentions are as important as capabilities, and the Soviet leadership misread American intentions in the early 1980s. Agents informing Project RYaN reported "facts" without context or interpretation. KGB analysts in Moscow were actively looking to confirm a hypothesis, not to explore the situation rationally.

Likewise, American leaders misread Soviet perceptions. Even with Reagan's aggressive rhetoric and 1983's unusually realistic war game scenario, the American intelligence community could not conceive that the USSR took the threat of a first strike seriously.

The way that the events of 1983 influenced Reagan's approach towards the Russians is as important as the economic pressure of Reagan's Star Wars defence programme when it comes to explaining why the Cold War ended. As Reagan later wrote in his memoirs, he had come to recognise that "Soviet officials feared us not only as adversaries but as potential aggressors who might hurl nuclear weapons at them in a first strike."

We Don't Need Nuclear Weapons

Marianne Hanson

In the following viewpoint, Dr. Marianne Hanson—reader in International Relations at the School of Political Science & International Studies at the University of Queensland—tackles the question of why nuclear warfare still remains a threat more than two decades after the end of the Cold War. In this speech given to a public forum on nuclear disarmament in 2009, Hanson systematically debunks five common arguments for the use of nuclear weapons and stresses the importance of fighting complacency and accepting the status quo.

Thank you very much, Richard, and good morning, ladies and gentlemen. As Richard said, I'm going to be addressing the topic of the myths, the continuing reasons that are put forward for why we apparently need nuclear weapons. Why is there still a belief among so many people that we need these nuclear weapons, that they actually serve a useful purpose? Well, let's just look at where we are at, at the moment. If nuclear weapons were primarily aimed at deterring the use of nuclear weapons between the superpowers during the Cold War, why is it that 20 years after the Cold War ended we still have around 25,000 or so of these weapons in existence, and many of them on hair-trigger alert?

Well, this is perhaps one of the most sobering examples of a human tendency to inertia, to complacency, of allowing the status quo to stand. It is after all easier to do nothing than to take the very active steps that are needed for real change. But this public

"Challenging the Myth That We Need Nuclear Weapons," by Marianne Hanson, Nautilus Institute, September 2009. Reprinted by Permission.

inertia...you're all exempted of course, but for the most part there seems to be a real sense of complacency.

But this isn't the only reason. This inertia is supported by persistent fears among governments and military figures that nuclear weapons are useful, that they must be kept. But this is built very much on a mindset, and Gareth Evans alluded to that mindset. It's a perception that these weapons actually still have a real utility and this is why they've got to be kept.

So what does this mindset consist of? I'm going to put forward five reasons; five main reasons that are generally listed as why we have to keep nuclear weapons, and then I'm going to address those.

1. We need nuclear weapons to deter wars between the major powers.
2. We need nuclear weapons to continue the purpose of nuclear deterrence, in other words to deter against others nuclear weapon use.
3. We need nuclear weapons to deter against chemical weapons or biological weapons attack, and especially terrorist attacks.
4. We need them as a security blanket in case of any future threat; a vague and ill-defined threat..."let's just keep them because we never know what's around the corner."
5. Well, we can't move to zero, we can't eliminate nuclear weapons because what if somebody cheats? In other words, we need a nuclear weapon to respond to what is called "breakout." In other words, if we were to get to the point of abolition, and a state or a sub-state group covertly designed and produced a nuclear weapon, how are we going to respond? Well, we better keep our nukes because that's the only way we're going to be able to respond to that factor of cheating or breakout.

All right, let's look at these in turn. First of all, that nuclear weapons are useful because they'll keep the peace between the major powers. Now, that might have been the case during the

Cold War. But in fact, there are very many other reasons why the major states did not go to war with each other, and are unlikely to go to war with each other now and in the future.

There is a range of economic and political reasons why the major powers are highly unlikely to go to war with each other today. We cannot really put forward the argument that it is nuclear weapons which have kept the peace in the past, and which are necessary for keeping the peace in the future.

The second argument, and this is related to that first one, that nuclear weapons are necessary to deter the use of other nuclear weapons. In other words, the deterrence argument, and others will be speaking on this at greater length later, but let me just address this very briefly.

Rolf Ekéus noted that the Canberra Commission and a number of other statements have said, well, there might be some continuing utility in this. In other words, as long as nuclear weapons exist, some states will feel that they need to retain their nuclear weapons so that they will deter the use of nuclear weapons against them.

But if we eliminate nuclear weapons, then this logic no longer holds, and it is a far better state to be in to have zero nuclear weapons than to continue to rely on the very unpredictable and indeed dangerous nature of nuclear weapons. So what we have here is a case or a reason that might still have some small utility, but which in fact there would be no logic in this once we reach the point of elimination.

What about the third reason I listed, that nuclear weapons are necessary to deter terrorist acts or chemical weapons attacks, biological weapons attacks. Well, the possession of nuclear weapons by the United States did nothing to deter the terrorist attacks on that country in 2001. The possession of nuclear weapons does not make a state secure.

We've seen far too many examples of where indeed a state can be attacked and has been attacked despite the possession of very large arsenals of nuclear weapons. In other words, possessing these weapons is no guarantee that a state can achieve security.

Moreover, keeping these weapons to respond to any such attack is equally fruitless.

Even if we were able to detect a terrorist cell, something which is in any case difficult to do, we don't need a nuclear weapon to respond to the threat of terrorism. We've seen in the past, indeed in the very recent past in Indonesia, conventional weapons have been used against terrorists.

The Federation of American Scientists, in a very well respected report, noted that if even a very, very small nuclear weapon, one of the bunker busters, had been used, let's say in Iraq to take out an alleged terrorist cell or to penetrate where there are suspected chemical or biological weapons, if these bunker busters, even one bunker buster had been used, we would likely have seen 25,000 civilian deaths.

Now, this is something that we are not prepared to accept. And no government in its right mind would contemplate the use of nuclear weapons to take out a terrorist cell, knowing that we are likely to have such high, such enormously high civilian casualties. We simply don't need a nuclear weapon to respond to terrorism.

The fourth argument is that we need to keep them as a security blanket against any sort of threat that might come up or might be a problem that we need to deal with at the moment or in the future. Well, what are the kinds of threats to security that we see at the moment?

We see the threat of environment degradation and climate change. We see economic meltdown. We see world hunger and poverty. We see the rise of piracy in certain parts of the world. Yes, these are all new threats to security or the threats that are defined as non-traditional security issues.

But can we say that nuclear weapons would be of any use whatsoever in addressing those threats? Clearly not. Nuclear weapons serve no purpose in responding not just to terrorism but to climate change, to global hunger, to economic crises and all of the other very real challenges that are posed today.

And then finally, the argument that we need nuclear weapons to respond to breakout or cheating. Again, using a nuclear weapon against a suspected state or sub state group that has built a nuclear weapon covertly where we have reached a position of zero nuclear weapons is simply not tenable. We have the conventional capabilities to respond to any such case of breakout. We do not need nuclear weapons to respond to any case of cheating in the future.

My conclusion then is that we really need to think carefully, and we need to challenge people who argue that we must have nuclear weapons, we must retain them because of the various reasons, some of which I've listed. We don't need them to respond to these challenges, and indeed as others have noted, keeping them only encourages other states to acquire them and continues the risk that they will one day be used, either deliberately or accidentally.

CHAPTER 2

The Major Players
in a Deadly Game

Preface

O nly opinions, but no answers, can legitimately serve as responses to the many questions surrounding the threat of nuclear war facing the world in the second decade of the twenty-first century. The dangers remain quite real more than seventy years after the first and only atomic weapons were dropped on Japan. One can argue that the most frightening prospects involve different countries than they did during the Cold War, which basically spotlighted only the United States, Soviet Union, and (to a lesser extent) China, but that does not make the planet any safer. The various issues regarding all the major players in this critical game of posturing, threatening, and international diplomacy will be discussed in this chapter.

The notion of mutually assured destruction (MAD) had been embraced in the 1950s and beyond as a reason to continue the arms race. The logic was that the more nuclear weapons that countries boasted in their stockpiles, the greater assurance that using them would destroy the enemy and, therefore, the less likely they were to be used. In the modern era, however, many have come to believe that is wishful thinking at best and that only the eventual elimination of nuclear weaponry can ensure the avoidance of catastrophe.

One major impetus for that line of thinking is based on optimism and hope. That is, the end of the Cold War has (at least until recently) thawed out relations between all the major powers. The possibility of a significant reduction in nuclear weaponry on all sides through diplomacy would seem to be a real one given the knowledge that spurred the MAD theory. The United States alone boasts enough firepower to destroy Russia many times over. That amount of weaponry has extended beyond what is necessary to reach mutually assured destruction.

But the focus has changed. The frightening prospect of nuclear arsenals falling into the wrong hands has gained the spotlight. Rogue nations with unstable and saber-rattling leaders such as Iran and North Korea seemingly pose a greater threat than Russia or China because their words and actions indicate they are just foolhardy enough to put their nuclear capabilities to bad use.

The scary prospect of a nuclear exchange had dissipated with the fall of the Soviet Union. But it has since returned. Chapter 2 will focus on where the world goes from here. There are no answers to give anyone clarity. The best that can be offered is speculation.

Preventing Nuclear War Without Disarming? Good Luck!

United Nations

The United Nations has been criticized for a perceived lack of muscle in world affairs and its inability to rein in the "bad guys" on the global stage. But the UN has often provided a moral compass for others to follow, as did the many speakers in its First Committee that are quoted in the following viewpoint. Strongly expressed here is the contention that mutually assured destruction (MAD) has no place in international thinking and diplomacy, and that trust and goodwill must supersede all else in dealing with the issue of nuclear proliferation.

Although nuclear weapons had not been engaged since 1945, the world "cannot rely on luck indefinitely," the First Committee (Disarmament and International Security) heard today as it continued its general debate.

The representative of Switzerland, noting that the United Nations had sought to eliminate nuclear weapons since its establishment, said it was everyone's responsibility to maintain that commitment.

Despite progress in some fields, he said, highlighting the Arms Trade Treaty, the use of nuclear rhetoric amid global tension and the inclusion of nuclear capabilities as part of military exercises were "worrying" developments.

More than four decades since the entry into force of the Treaty on the Non-Proliferation of Nuclear Weapons (NPT), non-nuclear-weapon States had a right to ask "if not now, when?" said New Zealand's representative.

Echoing sentiments expressed by the High Representative for Disarmament Affairs, she said that despite all that was wrong in the world—armed conflicts, arms races, and the orgy of military spending—disarmament did have a future and would survive for two reasons: it worked, and it was the right thing to do.

Disarmament did not happen in a vacuum, the representative of the Russian Federation said, adding that the future of that process depended to a great extent on the general security environment. Without the elimination of negative factors, the hopes for advancement towards "nuclear zero" would remain wishful thinking.

That representative also expressed concern about the concept of "prompt global strike," which was getting closer to the practical implementation phase. The goal was to immediately neutralize the defence capabilities of any "out-of-favour" country, leaving it without any time or opportunity for an armed response.

France's representative said that nuclear proliferation was a profound concern, and the European continent, which was thought to be permanently at peace, was once again prey to tensions. The Ukrainian crisis and the violation of the 1994 Budapest memorandum, adopted in the framework of Ukraine's accession to the NPT, had a "very negative effect" on international security, he said.

There was a sequence for multilateral action, with the entry into force of the Comprehensive Nuclear-Test-Ban Treaty (CTBT) and the launch of negotiations on a fissile material cut-off treaty, he said, adding that to make progress, it was essential to better understand each State's position, minimize divergences and identify possible avenues for compromise.

Sharing the worry of several delegations in the room, the representative of the Republic of Korea pointed out that, despite recent efforts, the possibility of nuclear terrorism remained a grave threat to international peace and security.

Brunei Darussalam's delegate added that the advancement of other weapons of mass destruction, particularly chemical and biological, were readily available in many countries and were now possible alternatives for terrorists. It was imperative, therefore, for the international community to ensure that counter-measures kept pace with the increasingly sophisticated methods for procuring such weapons.

Also speaking were the representatives of Belarus, Cuba, Israel, Mongolia, Malaysia, Algeria, Libya, Australia, Spain, Denmark and Senegal.

Exercising their right of reply were the representatives of Syria and Israel.

The First Committee will meet again at 10 a.m. tomorrow, 9 October, to continue its general debate.

Background

The First Committee (Disarmament and International Security) met this morning to continue its general debate on all related agenda items before it. For background, see Press Release GA/DIS/3497.

Statements

VALENTIN RYBAKOV, Deputy Minister for Foreign Affairs of Belarus, called for the universal adherence to the Nuclear Non-Proliferation Treaty (NPT), saying that, without the participation of all countries, the international community would remain far from reaching the goal of staunching proliferation. Implementation of the NPT had shown little progress to date, he said, pointing in particular to the lack of implementation of the 2010 NPT Review Conference Action Plan. Ahead of the 2015 NPT Review Conference, the international community must ensure that the outcome was not a "vague compromise" that merely reprinted the

2010 document. Instead, delegates must be courageous and work towards a specific framework.

Despite that, he said, the moratorium on nuclear testing was undoubtedly a step forward; however, it had a voluntary, *de facto* nature that made for a very fragile mechanism. Instead of relying on voluntary initiatives, the international community must aim for legally binding mechanisms. With that, he urged the entry into force of the Comprehensive Nuclear-Test-Ban Treaty (CTBT). To build a world free from nuclear tests, non-participating States must join the Treaty. Without universal participation, the CTBT could not be effective. Non-proliferation and the absence of nuclear tests were steps in the right direction, but were not an end in themselves. The ultimate goal should be the total, irreversible, elimination of nuclear and other weapons of mass destruction.

He noted that Belarus had been the first State in post-Soviet area to have renounced, voluntarily and without any precondition, possession of operational nuclear weapons deployed on its territory. In a similar vein, his country planned to table the traditional resolution on the prohibition of the development and manufacture of new types of weapons of mass destruction.

OSCAR LEÓN GONZÁLEZ (Cuba), supporting the statement made on behalf of the Non-Aligned Movement, urged the start of negotiations on a comprehensive convention on nuclear weapons to prohibit their production, stockpiling, transfer, and threat of use, and to stipulate their destruction. An international, high-level conference on the matter should be held no later than 2018, aimed at eliminating those weapons in the shortest possible timeframe. Cuba was proud to belong to the first densely populated area in the world to have declared itself nuclear-weapon free, through the Treaty for the Prohibition of Nuclear Weapons in Latin America and the Caribbean, known as the Treaty of Tlatelolco.

He said the only guarantee for the non-use of nuclear weapons was their full elimination and prohibition under strict international control. For that reason, it was unacceptable that deterrence remained the bedrock of military doctrines. Nuclear Powers continued to develop their arsenals via vertical proliferation, which was not highlighted enough by the international community. There remained a great distance between rhetoric and good intentions, as well as between commitments and the steps States were willing to take. A treaty should be concluded without delay to protect non-nuclear weapon States from the use, or threat of use, of nuclear weapons against them. It was also deeply unfortunate that a conference, as agreed, to establish a nuclear-weapon-free zone in the Middle East had not yet been held. The zone's establishment would be a monumental step forward in the peace process in that region. He reiterated the call for concrete steps towards the total elimination of nuclear weapons, adding that multilateral efforts were the only way to achieve that.

EYAL PROPPER, Deputy Head of the Division for Strategic Affairs at the Ministry of Foreign Affairs of Israel, said that the Middle East lacked mechanisms to foster dialogue and greater understanding between regional players. Because of the refusal of some countries to recognize Israel, there were no processes that could contribute to building confidence, de-escalation of tensions and conflict resolution. He lamented the lack of forums for direct communication between the States of the region, able to address core security issues and encourage the attainment of solutions. The Middle East had distinguished itself by blatant violations and a lack of respect for formal treaty obligations. Within the context of the NPT, four out of five violations had occurred to date in his region, notably in Iran, Syria, Libya and Iraq. Dialogue was essential to achieve peace and security in the region, and urged a "pragmatic and realistic approach".

Israel, for its part, had reiterated its willingness to participate in a sixth round of consultations, convened by the Finnish Under-Secretary, to discuss the conditions necessary for establishing a Middle East zone free of weapons of mass destruction, he said. Regretfully, however, there was a "significant conceptual gap" between regional States on fundamental security concepts. While Israel had sought a consensus-based approach, its neighbours had yet to adopt the same pragmatism. In their efforts to impose such a zone, Arab countries refused to engage Israel directly and establish a path towards convening a conference in Helsinki.

He went on to state that Iran remained the "cardinal threat" to the region's security. In its unrelenting pursuit of developing nuclear-weapon capability and advancing its regional ambitions, the country supported terrorist organizations with the supply of weapons, financing and training. He warned that the election of the "so-called moderates" in Iran and the emergence of the Islamic State in Iraq and the Levant/Sham (ISIL/ISIS) should not lead the international community to underestimate the threat still posed by Iran. That country participated in processes such as the "E3+3" talks to alleviate pressures and "buy more time" for development of its military programme, he alleged. There was still no clear indication of the country's intention to curb its nuclear capabilities, as demanded by several Security Council resolutions.

MIKHAIL ULYANOV (Russian Federation) said that the elimination of the threat posed by weapons of mass destruction, including nuclear weapons, remained one of the international community's key priorities. The Russian Federation was actively working in that direction by taking concrete steps to limit and reduce nuclear arsenals. Over the past 25 years, those stocks had been reduced "manifold," and under the new START treaty, his country had set out a goal to reach the agreed aggregate levels of warheads, delivery means and launchers by early 2018, which was achievable. The Intermediate-Range Nuclear Forces Treaty (INF Treaty) of 1987, between the Russian Federation and the United States, also remained in effect. However, Russia's "American partners" had committed "gross and massive" violations of that instrument's obligations. He hoped, as a result of the dialogue on those issues, that the United States would return to full compliance with that important accord.

Disarmament did not happen in a vacuum, he said, as the future of that process depended to a great extent on the general security environment. Without the elimination of negative factors, the hopes for advancement towards "nuclear zero" would remain wishful thinking. His delegation had growing concerns about the concept of "prompt global strike," which was getting closer to the practical implementation phase. The goal was to immediately neutralize the defence capabilities of any "out of favour" country, leaving it without any time or opportunity for an armed response. Such research efforts were even riskier when undertaken in the context of the policy towards establishing one's exclusiveness and overwhelming military supremacy.

Regarding "nuclear sharing" among the North Atlantic Treaty Organization (NATO) countries, in which non-nuclear members of the alliance accepted nuclear weapons on their territory and participated in the planning of their use, he said that was incompatible, with either the letter or spirit of the NPT. That Treaty's article I prohibited the transfer of nuclear weapons to any recipient whatsoever, directly or indirectly. He called on NATO members to bring their policy into compliance with their obligations.

Turning to the "chemical demilitarization" in Syria, he said that had been one of the major achievements in the area of weapons of mass destruction non-proliferation and disarmament. Syrian authorities had eliminated chemical arsenals under unprecedentedly difficult conditions and were in full compliance with their obligations. Thus, the so-called "Syrian chemical dossier" was no longer an urgent matter, and should be considered under regular procedures of the Organisation of the Prohibition of Chemical Weapons.

OH JOON, Republic of Korea, said that the CTBT's entry into force and negotiations on a fissile material cut-off treaty remained the two most urgent tasks to be tackled together by the international community. His country urged the remaining eight "Annex 2" States, whose ratification was required for the Nuclear-Test-Ban Treaty's entry into force, to do so without delay. He also reiterated his country's long-standing call for the commencement of negotiations on a fissile material ban in the Geneva-based

Conference on Disarmament, and was hopeful that the Group of Governmental Experts could pave the way forward.

He said that, despite recent efforts, the possibility of nuclear terrorism remained a grave threat to international peace and security. Building upon the landmark Washington and Seoul Summits, the 2014 Hague Nuclear Security Summit was a crucial step forward in global efforts to prevent such activities. As the host of the 2012 Summit, his country would continue to work with others in establishing a robust and enduring nuclear security architecture. The United Nations had an important role to play, he said, stressing that Member States should step up their efforts to achieve the full and universal implementation of Security Council resolution 1540 (2004), which aimed to prevent the transfer of mass destruction weapons to terrorists.

Another serious threat to international peace and security was the Democratic People's Republic of Korea's continued development of nuclear weapon and ballistic missile programmes, he said, noting that the "DPRK" was the only country in the twenty-first century that had conducted nuclear tests. Further development of its nuclear capabilities continued, and the "DPRK" was now threatening a new form of nuclear testing. Already, the international community had condemned the ballistic missiles it had launched this year as clear violations of Security Council resolutions. As such, the world must send a clear and united message to that country that, under no circumstances, could it become a nuclear-weapon State and that subsequent tests by the country would be met with serious consequences.

JEAN-HUGUES SIMON-MICHEL (France) expressed "immense satisfaction" that the Arms Trade Treaty had now passed the necessary threshold for entry into force at the end of this year. Crises continued around the world, and, in some cases, were breaking out anew, such as in the Middle East, Central African Republic, Libya and Iraq. The effects of those conflicts were felt even in Europe, and were a reminder that "we live in the real world" and that the approach to disarmament and arms control should be realistic. Nuclear proliferation remained a central concern, and the European continent, which was thought to be permanently at peace, was once again prey to tensions. The Ukrainian crisis and the violation of the 1994 Budapest memorandum, adopted in the framework of Ukraine's accession to the NPT, had a "very negative effect" on international security.

Yet, despite the degradation of the international strategic context, disarmament and arms control had made progress in 2014, he said. In addition to the Arms Trade Treaty, there was also the success of the Maputo review conference of the Anti-Personnel Mine Ban Convention, and pragmatic solutions had been proposed to address the problem of space debris. However, nuclear-weapon States needed to "be equal to their commitments," and France was aware of its responsibilities in that respect. The road map agreed at the 2010 NPT Review Conference constituted a common approach that committed all States parties to a "step-by-step" approach. There was a sequence for multilateral action, with the entry into force of the CTBT and the launch of negotiations on a fissile material cut-off treaty. To make progress, it was essential to better understand each State's position, minimize divergences and identify possible avenues for compromise. France's aim remained, more than ever, to move on to the next stage and begin negotiations; debates held this year at the Conference on Disarmament were moving things in that direction. The step-by-step approach was the only realistic path and would allow determined pursuit of a safer world.

OD OCH (Mongolia) agreed with previous speakers that the NPT was the cornerstone of the nuclear disarmament and non-proliferation regime, and an "essential part of the global security regime" overall. Mongolia joined the call on all States parties to "spare no effort" in achieving the Treaty's universality. The full and effective implementation of all provisions was required to preserve its relevance, effectiveness and credibility. As a strong advocate of nuclear-weapon-free zones, Mongolia was concerned about the lack of implementation of the 1995 Middle East resolution, but was hopeful that international efforts would yield progress in establishing such a zone in the Middle East.

He went on to state that Mongolia—recognizing the Conference on Disarmament as the single, multilateral, negotiating body on disarmament—was hopeful, as its co-chair in 2015, that the necessary political will would be created to ensure the commencement of substantive work. Looking ahead, innovative approaches must be explored to make possible the resumption of meaningful disarmament negotiations. On the CTBT, Mongolia stressed the importance of maintaining a moratorium on all types of nuclear weapon tests; however, unless the Treaty was legally binding, it would remain fragile. It was for that reason Mongolia joined the Joint Ministerial Statement on the CTBT to speed up ratifications.

The potential spread of weapons of mass destruction and their delivery means constituted a threat to international peace and security, he said, adding that, as a result, Mongolia has been undertaking efforts to promote the non-proliferation of weapons of mass destruction by joining all major international frameworks and abiding by its obligation under relevant agreements.

BENNO LAGGNER (Switzerland) said that preventing the proliferation of nuclear weapons and achieving a world free of those weapons must remain the objective of steadfast pursuit by the international community. The United Nations had sought their elimination since the Organization's establishment, and it was everyone's responsibility to maintain that commitment. His delegation was deeply concerned by the slow pace of nuclear disarmament, the lack of decisive change in nuclear doctrines and the qualitative development of those weapons. The use of nuclear rhetoric amid international tension and the inclusion of nuclear capabilities as part of military exercises, as well as questions on the future of the INF Treaty, were all worrying developments and a reminder that, although nuclear weapons had not been engaged since 1945, the world "cannot rely on luck indefinitely."

He said that conferences on the humanitarian impact of nuclear weapons had clearly demonstrated that the explosion of a single such weapon would have catastrophic consequences. All States should take part in those summits, because nuclear weapons affected all. He sought greater efforts to further implementation of the 2010 NPT Action Plan, and dossiers as essential as the establishment of a zone free of nuclear and other weapons of mass destruction in the Middle East. Regarding the conflict in Syria, he welcomed efforts made to guarantee the neutralization of chemical weapons stockpiles; however, he remained extremely concerned about the interim conclusions of the Organisation for the Prohibition of Chemical Weapons' (OPCW) fact-finding mission that toxic chemicals had been used repeatedly in Syria.

While mass destruction weapons required immediate attention, he said in closing, conventional weapons still claimed numerous victims each year. As such, the rapid entry into force of the Arms Trade Treaty was crucial.

HUSSEIN HANIFF (Malaysia), said that greater public awareness was required on the issue of nuclear disarmament, with more attention paid to the calls of civil society. "Fresh perspectives and innovative approaches" should be considered by expanding the number of stakeholders in the disarmament discourse. That could provide opportunities for achieving the desired changes. Government representatives must live up to their commitments. For its part, Malaysia reaffirmed its commitment to pursue a world free of nuclear weapons, as embodied in the NPT. On that note, he emphasized the urgent need to convene a conference on a zone free of nuclear and other weapons of mass destruction in the Middle East.

On the Conference on Disarmament, he said that the priorities must be rationalized in that consideration of one issue should not be a precondition for proceeding on another. Nor should members be fixated on the consensus rule. Instead, efforts should focus on constructive proposals for improving the Conference's working methods. As its president in 2014, Malaysia would present the report and the draft resolution to the First Committee during the cluster on disarmament machinery. While the Conference worked to overcome its impasse, Malaysia remained convinced that a convention on nuclear weapons was long overdue. In 2007, his country, together with Costa Rica, had submitted a model nuclear weapons convention to the General Assembly, which set out legal, technical and political elements for rendering the world nuclear-weapon-free. As such, his country stood ready to work with other Member States on the model convention, or on any other proposal that would bring the world closer to that goal.

SABRI BOUKADOUM (Algeria), associating himself with the Arab Group, African Union and Non-Aligned Movement, said that effective steps and substantive progress in the area of disarmament remained elusive. Nuclear disarmament was Algeria's highest priority, out of concern for the dangers those weapons posed to humanity. His country was committed to the NPT as the cornerstone of the nuclear disarmament and non-proliferation regime, but it must be universalized. Nuclear-weapon States had the primary responsibility to achieve nuclear disarmament, and he called for effective implementation of General Assembly resolution 68/32, including the urgent commencement of negotiations in the Conference on Disarmament for the early conclusion of a comprehensive convention on nuclear weapons to prohibit their possession, development, production, acquisition, testing, stockpiling, transfer, use or threat of use and to provide for their destruction.

Noting that a majority of NPT States parties had chosen to use atomic energy for exclusively civilian applications in line with the Treaty's article IV, he said that, for many developing countries, nuclear energy represented a strategic choice for their economic development and energy security needs. Accordingly, Algeria reaffirmed the legitimate right to develop, research and use nuclear energy for peaceful purposes. He noted that his country had been among the first to sign the African Nuclear-Weapon-Free Zone Treaty, or Pelindaba Treaty, but he regretted that a conference to create such a zone in the Middle East had not yet been held. With regard to the Conference on Disarmament, he said the continuing impasse was a result of a lack of political will. To address that deadlock, he urged the convening of a fourth special session of the General Assembly.

On conventional weapons, he said that the illicit trade of small arms and light weapons continued to threaten the peace and stability of many countries and regions. That illicit trade, particularly in North Africa and the Sahel region, involved the supply of arms to terrorist groups and organized crime networks. Thus, the United Nations Programme of Action and the International Tracing Instrument were more than ever of the utmost relevance.

IBRAHIM O. A. DABBASHI (Libya) said that his country sought the elimination of weapons of mass destruction and believed that the total elimination of nuclear weapons was the only guarantee that they would not be used in the future. In 2003, Libya had renounced its programme on nuclear and other weapons of mass destruction, and had also pledged to eliminate chemical weapons by 2015. Libya was hopeful that other States would follow in its footsteps and urged, in particular, nuclear-weapon States to honour the NPT.

Libya welcomed the adoption of General Assembly resolution 68/32 on nuclear disarmament and believed that implementation of all of its provisions would make it effective towards achieving the complete elimination of nuclear weapons. Non-adherence to existing instruments was a threat to international peace, he said, noting that Libya favoured a convention on nuclear weapons as that could pave the way for a nuclear-weapon free zone in the Middle East. Pending that, however, the international community must put pressure on Israel as the only country in the region that was not a party to the NPT. He went on to stress the importance of the universality of the CTBT, which could help achieve the "noble goal" of ridding the world of nuclear weapons.

Libya respected the right of NPT States parties to produce nuclear energy for peaceful purposes, adding, however, that a balance must be maintained with the important commitments outlined in the Treaty. Libya also supported nuclear-weapon-free zones in all four corners of the world and called on all parties to redouble their efforts to implement the outcomes of the 1995 NPT Review and Extension Conference. He stressed that there was a vital need to revitalize the Conference on Disarmament, which had an important role to play as a negotiating platform in nuclear disarmament. On conventional weapons, Libya had signed the Arms Trade Treaty to help prevent the infiltration of those weapons in civil conflicts around the world.

DELL HIGGIE (New Zealand) said that implementing the Arms Trade Treaty would prove key to reaping the human security and development outcomes expected to flow from it. All could be heartened by the Treaty's success story, which, thanks to civil society's ongoing support and attentive eye, would continue to go from strength to strength. Less heartening, however, was the lack of progress on the First Committee's key item, namely, nuclear disarmament. Not all United Nations Member States based their approaches to nuclear weapons issues on the NPT, but an overwhelming number of States did so, in steadfast support of that Treaty as the cornerstone of their disarmament and non-proliferation policies. Yet, unfinished business remained. More than four decades since the NPT entered into force, non-nuclear-weapon States had a right to ask: "if not now, when?"

She stressed the need for human security, rather than war strategies, to be at the core of the international community's deliberations on nuclear weapons issues. Wishing to draw from the optimism of the United Nations High Representative for Disarmament Affairs, Angela Kane, she echoed the sentiment that, despite all that was wrong in the world—armed conflicts, arms races, and the orgy of military spending—disarmament did have a future and would survive for two reasons: it worked, and it was the right thing to do.

SHARMAN STONE, (Australia), said that the past year had seen important progress in the implementation of the Convention

CHINA TESTS ITS MOST DANGEROUS NUCLEAR WEAPON OF ALL TIME

China conducted a flight test of its new intercontinental ballistic missile (ICBM) this month.

This week, Bill Gertz reported that earlier this month, China conducted the fourth flight test of its DF-41 road-mobile ICBM.

"The DF-41, with a range of between 6,835 miles and 7,456 miles, is viewed by the Pentagon as Beijing's most potent nuclear missile and one of several new long-range missiles in development or being deployed," Gertz reports.

He goes on to note that this is the fourth time in the past three years that China has tested the DF-41, indicating that the missile is nearing deployment. Notably, according to Gertz, in the latest test China shot two independently targetable warheads from the DF-41, further confirming that the DF-41 will hold multiple independently targetable reentry vehicles (MIRV).

As I've noted before, China's acquisition of a MIRVed capability is one of the most dangerous nuclear weapons developments that no one is talking about.

MIRVed missiles carry payloads of several nuclear warheads each capable of being directed at a different set of targets. They are considered extremely destabilizing to the strategic balance primarily because they place a premium on striking first and create a "use em or lose em" nuclear mentality.

Along with being less vulnerable to anti-ballistic missile systems, this is true for two primary reasons. First, and most obviously, a single MIRVed missile can be used to eliminate numerous enemy nuclear sites simultaneously. Thus, theoretically at least, only a small portion of an adversary's missile force would be necessary to completely eliminate one's strategic deterrent. Secondly, MIRVed missiles enable countries to use cross-targeting techniques of employing two or more missiles against a single target, which increases the kill probability. In other words, MIRVs are extremely destabilizing because they make adversary's nuclear arsenals vulnerable to being wiped out in a surprise first strike.

China's acquisition of a MIRVed capability is also likely to upset the strategic balance with Russia. As Moscow's conventional military capabilities have eroded since the fall of the Soviet Union, Russia has leaned more heavily on nuclear weapons for its national defense. It therefore seeks to maintain a clear nuclear advantage over potential adversaries like China. Beijing's acquisition of MIRVed missiles threatens to erode this advantage.

— "China **Tests Its Most Dangerous Nuclear Weapon of All Time**," by Zachary Keck, August 19, 2015.

on Cluster Munitions and the Mine Ban Convention. Citing the tragic impact on civilians of cluster munitions and anti-personnel mines, Australia urged adherence to international norms established by those Conventions and welcomed the recent United States' announcement of further changes to more closely align the country's activities "outside the Korean peninsula" with the key requirements of the Mine Ban Convention.

In order to remove the threat of nuclear war, it was incumbent upon all to diminish the utility of those weapons, she said, adding that the starting point of the disarmament process must be the inclusion of nuclear-armed States. Some, including the United States and Russian Federation, have made considerable reductions in their nuclear arsenals, and yet, with more than 16,000 nuclear weapons in the hands of nine States, "much more needs to be done." There could be no short-cuts to create the conditions necessary for a world without nuclear weapons, and to that end, Australia and fellow members of the Non-Proliferation and Disarmament Initiative (NPDI) proposed practical steps to contribute to greater nuclear transparency and further reductions. It welcomed the recent report regarding the NPT, but sought more detail and transparency in those documents.

Another priority of Australia was the entry into force of the Test-Ban Treaty, she said, noting that, last month, her country had co-hosted a ministerial meeting, which committed to a strong statement of support for the Treaty's prompt entry into force. Along with Mexico and New Zealand, Australia would present the annual CTBT resolution during this year's First Committee session, and she invited broad support to reinforce the need to maintain a testing moratorium.

MARIA VICTORIA GONZÁLEZ ROMÁN (Spain), associating with the European Union, said that in the past few years the international community had made several achievements in two important areas of disarmament, the nuclear and conventional weapons realms. Progress was still needed in other areas, however, including in the Conference on Disarmament and the inability to begin negotiations on a fissile material cut-off treaty. Still, the adoption of the Arms Trade Treaty was a milestone in the field of international relations, and the control of arms exports was now linked to human rights and the need to maintain peace, stability and international security.

The comprehensive development of the NPT entailed progress in the compliance with article VI, she said, welcoming the bilateral agreements between the United States and the Russian Federation to reduce their strategic nuclear weapons. The CTBT would surely be another fundamental component in the disarmament and non-proliferation architecture, when it entered into force. She called on States that had not yet signed or ratified the Treaty, in particular Annex 2 States, to do so as soon as possible. She highlighted the importance for compliance by the Democratic People's Republic of Korea with Security Council resolutions, and urged it to negotiate in good faith an agreement that would banish the nuclear threat from the Korean peninsula. She supported efforts under way to reach a diplomatic solution in the case of Iran, and welcomed the collaboration that had characterized the negotiations which began last November. Finally, she underscored the importance of strengthening security in the face of possible biological threats, be they natural, accidental or criminal.

[…]

Rogue Nations and Nuclear Peril

John R. Bolton

Though the following piece was written in 2003, the author already recognized the growing threat and danger of rogue nations such as North Korea and Iran gaining nuclear capability. Bolton, who had served as under secretary for arms control and international security, expressed his view at the Conference of the Institute for Foreign Policy Analysis and the Fletcher Schools International Security Studies Program that unstable regimes that become nuclear capable pose the most significant threat to world security.

John R. Bolton, Under Secretary for Arms Control and International Security

Remarks to the Conference of the Institute for Foreign Policy Analysis and the Fletcher Schools International Security Studies Program

Washington, DC

December 2, 2003

It is a real pleasure to have the opportunity to be here at the Institute for Foreign Policy Analysis to discuss the risks we face from nuclear weapons in the hands of rogue states, and the steps the Bush Administration is taking to deal with those threats. Progress by terrorist states towards a nuclear weapons capability, while often slow and uncertain, concealed and camouflaged, must nonetheless engage American attention in a sustained and systematic fashion. Often undertaken in conjunction with ambitious ballistic missile programs, efforts to attain nuclear weapons pose a direct and

"Nuclear Weapons and Rogue States: Challenge and Response," by John R. Bolton, State. gov, December 2, 2003.

undeniable threat to the United States and its friends and allies around the world. Whether the nuclear capabilities of states like Iran, North Korea and others are threats today, or "only" threats "tomorrow," there can be no dispute that our attention is required now before the threats become reality, and tens of thousands of innocent civilians, or more, have been vaporized.

This is not to say by any means that we should not also be gravely concerned about chemical and biological weapons programs. We are, and many of the steps that we take internationally against nuclear weapons are applicable to chemical and biological threats as well. In fact, states around the world are closely scrutinizing the way we deal with the proliferation of nuclear weapons, and you can be sure that they will draw the appropriate conclusions about the utility of other weapons of mass destruction (WMD) based on our performance in the nuclear field.

Of course, our information about WMD programs in other countries is not perfect. No one is more aware of the uncertainties that we face than the senior American intelligence officials and policy makers who deal with these life-and-death issues. Some analysts have said that not finding WMD in Iraq—to date—proves that Saddam was not an imminent threat, and that our Coalition military action was therefore not justified. These criticisms miss the mark that our concern was not the imminence of Saddam's threat, but the very existence of his regime, given its heinous and undeniable record, capabilities, intentions, and longstanding defiance of the international community. President Bush specifically and unambiguously addressed this issue in his January 2003, State of the Union message when he said: "Some have said we must not act until the threat is imminent. Since when have terrorists and tyrants announced their intentions, politely putting us on notice before they strike? If this threat is permitted to fully and suddenly emerge, all actions, all words, and all recriminations would come too late. Trusting in the sanity and restraint of Saddam Hussein is not a strategy, and it is not an option."

Given the right opportunity or incentive, Saddam could have easily transferred WMD capabilities to terrorist groups or others for their use against us, with potentially catastrophic results. State sponsors of terrorism are aggressively working to acquire weapons of mass destruction and their missile delivery systems. While Saddam's removal from power has unquestionably improved the international security situation, we face significant challenges in other parts of the world. Rogue states such as Iran, North Korea, Syria, Libya and Cuba, whose pursuit of weapons of mass destruction makes them hostile to U.S. interests, will learn that their covert programs will not escape either detection or consequences. While we will pursue diplomatic solutions whenever possible, the United States and its allies are also willing to deploy more robust techniques, such as the interdiction and seizure of illicit goods. If rogue states are not willing to follow the logic of nonproliferation norms, they must be prepared to face the logic of adverse consequences. It is why we repeatedly caution that no option is off the table.

Iran

Let me discuss two problems in particular: Iran and North Korea. Although Iran has biological, chemical and missile programs, I will focus today on their nuclear weapons program, which Iran itself has acknowledged has been underway for at least eighteen years—all in violation of Iran's obligations under the Nuclear Nonproliferation Treaty ("NPT"). Our strategy for nearly three years has been to use bilateral and multilateral pressure to end that program, and to secure international consensus against Iran's pursuit of a nuclear weapons capability. On November 26, the International Atomic Energy Agency ("IAEA") Board of Governors unanimously adopted a resolution that "strongly deplores Iran's past failures and breaches of its obligations to comply with the provisions of its Safeguards Agreement...." There was also unanimous agreement that "should any further serious Iranian failures come to light, the Board of Governors would meet immediately to consider . . . all options at its disposal, in accordance with the IAEA Statute and Iran's Safeguards Agreement."

This decisive action followed three successive reports by the IAEA's Director General, which established beyond doubt Iran's multiple violations. While Iran has consistently denied any program to develop nuclear weapons, the IAEA has amassed an enormous amount of evidence to the contrary that makes this denial increasingly implausible.

In what can only be an attempt to build a capacity to develop nuclear materials for nuclear weapons, Iran has enriched uranium with both centrifuges and lasers, and produced and reprocessed plutonium. It attempted to cover its tracks by repeatedly and over many years neglecting to report its activities, and in many instances providing false declarations to the IAEA. For example, the IAEA Director General reports that Iran conducted uranium enrichment experiments with centrifuges using uranium Iran told the IAEA was "lost" due to its leaking valves. Iran conducted unreported uranium conversion experiments with uranium Iran declared to the IAEA as process loss. And Iran delayed IAEA inspectors until key facilities had been sanitized.

I repeat: The United States believes that the longstanding, massive and covert Iranian effort to acquire sensitive nuclear capabilities make sense only as part of a nuclear weapons program. Iran is trying to legitimize as "peaceful and transparent" its pursuit of nuclear fuel cycle capabilities that would give it the ability to produce fissile material for nuclear weapons. This includes uranium mining and extraction, uranium conversion and enrichment, reactor fuel fabrication, heavy water production, a heavy water reactor well-suited for plutonium production, and the "management" of spent fuel—a euphemism for reprocessing spent fuel to recover plutonium. The IAEA Director General's report confirms that Iran has been engaged in all of these activities over many years, and that it deliberately and repeatedly lied to the IAEA about it.

The international community now needs to decide over time whether Iran has come clean on this program and how to react to the large number of serious violations to which Iran has admitted. Unfortunately, Iran itself has already indicated that it has mixed feelings about its obligations to adhere to the IAEA's resolutions. Last Saturday, Hasan Rowhani, head of Iran's Supreme National Security Council and the man who concluded the October deal in Tehran with the three European foreign ministers, gave Iran's most recent interpretation of the IAEA's actions. He said, "Our decision to suspend uranium enrichment is voluntary and temporary. Uranium enrichment is Iran's natural right and [Iran] will reserve for itself this right....There has been and there will be no question of a permanent suspension or halt at all." Rowhani went on to say, "We want to control the whole fuel cycle. Since we are planning to build seven nuclear fuel plants in the future, we want to provide fuel for at least one of the plants ourselves."

The IAEA's November 26 resolution should leave no doubt that one more transgression by Iran will mean that the IAEA is obligated to report Iran's noncompliance to the Security Council and General Assembly of the United Nations, in accordance with Article XII.C of the IAEA Statute. This Statute explicitly states that when non-compliance is found, the "Board shall report the non-compliance to all members and to the Security Council." Iran's Safeguards Agreement similarly provides that if the Board finds "the Agency is not able to verify there has been no diversion of nuclear material required to be safeguarded," the Board may report to the Security Council. The real issue now is whether the Board of Governors will remain together in its insistence that Iran's pursuit of nuclear weapons is illegitimate, or whether Iranian efforts to split the Board through economic incentives and aggressive propaganda will succeed. For our part, the United States will continue its efforts to prevent the transfer of sensitive nuclear and ballistic missile technology to Iran, from whatever source, and will monitor the situation there with great care.

North Korea

With regard to North Korea, President Bush's objective is quite clear: the United States seeks the complete, verifiable, and irreversible dismantlement of North Korea's nuclear programs. We seek to bring this about, as we have said repeatedly, through diplomatic dialogue in a multilateral framework involving those states with the most direct stakes in the outcome. Other states may yet be involved as appropriate. The North Korean nuclear program is not a bilateral issue between the United States and the DPRK. It is a profound challenge to regional stability, and to the global nuclear nonproliferation regime.

We look forward to the earliest resumption of the next round of six-party talks. Secretary Powell has repeatedly emphasized a special thanks to the People's Republic of China for the work that they have done to encourage North Korea to come to the negotiating table. At those talks, we hope to make tangible progress toward the goal of a nuclear weapons-free North Korea. We are prepared to provide a written document on security assurances to Pyongyang with other participants in the talks. Such assurances can only be provided, however, in the context of agreement and implementation of an effective verification regime that would provide assurances to us that the DPRK will not reconstitute its nuclear program. For the United States, irreversibility is a paramount goal.

We are determined that bad behavior on the part of North Korea will not be rewarded. North Korea will not be given inducements to reverse actions it took in violation of its treaty commitments and other international obligations. Moreover, attempts to delay or postpone the six-party talks simply because one or more of the parties wishes to raise issues of vital concern should be rejected. Japan, for example, feels strongly that it should have the right at least to raise the issue of North Korean abductions of Japanese citizens over the years. For Japan, this is a fundamental issue, and Japan's desire to raise it should be respected. Japan's participation in the six-party process is essential. Whether North Korea yet understands these fundamental precepts of American policy remains to be seen.

As in the case of Iran, of course, the Security Council is another logical venue in which to discuss the threat to international peace and security represented by the DPRK's nuclear weapons program. To date, China, supported by Russia, has argued that the DPRK issue is better handled in the six-party context rather than the Security Council, and we have agreed. Similarly, France, the United Kingdom and others urged recently that the case of Iran not be reported to the Security Council, and we agreed to that, too. Of course, we hope that the other four Permanent Members of the Security Council are aware of the long-term implications of these decisions, as we are. Policies intended to bring about the termination of the Iranian and DPRK nuclear weapons programs, which result in reducing the Council's role under the Charter, would be truly unfortunate and ironic.

The Proliferation Security Initiative

To roll back the proliferation activities of rogue states and to ensure that their WMD progress is not passed on to terrorist groups or their state sponsors, the United States employs a variety of diplomatic and other methods. President Bush announced our newest and most promising effort, the Proliferation Security Initiative ("PSI"), on May 31 in Krakow, Poland. The United States and ten other close allies and friends have worked to develop this initiative, which seeks to combat proliferation by developing new means to disrupt WMD trafficking at sea, in the air, and on land. Our goal is to create a more robust approach to preventing WMD, missiles, and related technologies flowing to and from would-be proliferators.

The PSI has been a fast-moving effort, reflecting the urgency attached to establishing a more coordinated and active basis to prevent proliferation. On September 4, we published the PSI "Statement of Interdiction Principles" and shared it with countries around the world. More than 50 countries have

UN SANCTIONS AGAINST IRAN

In 1979, at the time of the Islamic revolution and the hostage crisis, the United States imposed broad economic sanctions against Iran. Since then, Washington has imposed various additional sanctions against Tehran, accusing the Iranian government of developing nuclear weapons and sponsoring or funding terrorism abroad.

In February 2003, Iran revealed its uranium enrichment program at Natanz, claiming it was using the technology for peaceful purposes and inviting the UN nuclear monitoring body, the International Atomic Energy Agency (IAEA), to visit. The US, however, alleged that the program is part of a drive to develop nuclear weapons and sought to refer the Iranian case to the Security Council. However in November 2004, Tehran signed a temporary agreement with Germany, France and Britain to cease uranium enrichment and the IAEA issued Iran a clean bill of health, effectively avoiding Security Council intervention. Nevertheless, the IAEA said it could not confirm that Iran was not pursuing undeclared nuclear activities and referred the case to the UN Security Council.

In June 2006, the Security Council adopted a resolution endorsing the P5 and Germany offer of diplomatic and economic incentives and demanding that Iran suspend all uranium enrichment programs by August 31. In December 2006, after Tehran's failure to comply, the Council imposed sanctions on Iran's trade in sensitive nuclear materials and technology. Following the IAEA's offer to Tehran of a 60-day grace period where halting of the country's uranium enrichment would be exchanged for suspension of UN sanctions which Iran did not take up, the Security Council passed Resolution 1747 in March 2007, intensifying the previous sanctions package while also naming specific officials as targets of the sanctions and adding additional sanctions against Iranian financial institutions.

Nevertheless, Iran vowed to continue enriching uranium, citing its right to do so without external interference and within the limits of international law. Indeed, Iran has demonstrated compliance with the Nuclear Non-Proliferation Treaty (NPT), and the countries that have backed sanctions have provided no evidence to the contrary.

Although the Security Council may soon vote on a resolution, Council members such as Brazil, Turkey and Lebanon advocate continued diplomacy. The sanctions that have been slapped on Iran have not made the Iranian government more responsive to the demands of the Security Council and the IAEA. However, these sanctions have caused Iranian civilians much hardship, once again calling into question the legitimacy of general and targeted sanctions.

—**"UN Sanctions Against Iran," Global Policy Forum.**

signaled that they support the PSI and are ready to participate in interdiction efforts.

To date, PSI participants have agreed on a series of ten sea, air, and ground interdiction training exercises. Four have already taken place, and the remaining exercises will occur in the coming months. Australia conducted the first exercise in October in the Coral Sea, involving both military and law enforcement assets. The United Kingdom then hosted the first PSI air interception training session, a table-top exercise to explore operational issues arising from intercepting proliferation traffic in the air. In mid-October, Spain hosted the second maritime exercise, this one in the western Mediterranean Sea. Finally, France recently hosted a third maritime exercise in the Mediterranean Sea. PSI nations have now trained for maritime interdictions in both the Mediterranean and the western Pacific Ocean, two areas that are particularly prone to proliferation trafficking.

The eleven original PSI participants are now involving additional countries in PSI activities. Last month, the Japanese Government hosted a meeting to inform Asian governments about PSI and encourage their cooperation in interdiction efforts. There was broad support among the governments that further efforts needed to be undertaken to stop proliferation and that they would study the PSI as a new tool for addressing nonproliferation.

Later this month, the United States will host the fifth PSI operational experts meeting, which will bring together military and law enforcement experts from the original eleven participating countries, as well as Norway, Denmark, Singapore, and Canada. Since PSI is an "activity" rather than an "organization," the meeting will develop military and law enforcement capabilities and preparations for interdictions.

As the PSI moves forward, we expect other countries will join in training exercises to enhance global capabilities to respond quickly when governments receive intelligence on proliferation shipments. President Bush has made clear that our long-term objective is to create a web of counterproliferation partnerships through which proliferators will have difficulty carrying out their trade in WMD and missile-related technology. As the President said, "We're determined to keep the world's most destructive weapons away from all our shores, and out of the hands of our common enemies."

Our PSI interdiction efforts rest on existing domestic and international authorities. The national legal authorities of each participant will allow us to act together in a flexible manner, ensuring actions are taken by participants with the most robust authorities in any given case. By coordinating our efforts with other countries, we draw upon an enhanced set of authorities for interdiction. At the December operational meeting, legal experts will analyze their authorities against real world scenarios and examine any gaps in authorities that can be filled either through national legislation or policy or international action. Experts also will work to enhance our ability to share information with law enforcement and military operators in a timely and effective manner, in order to allow operators to increase the number of actual interdictions.

Properly planned and executed, the interception of critical technologies can prevent hostile states and terrorists from acquiring these dangerous capabilities. At a minimum, interdiction can lengthen the time that proliferators will need to acquire new weapons capabilities, increase their cost, and demonstrate our resolve to combat proliferation.

Conclusion

Our initiatives move us closer to a more secure world where we are able not only to impede the spread of WMD, but also to "roll back" and ultimately eliminate such weapons from the arsenals of rogue states and ensure that the terrorist groups they sponsor do not acquire a shortcut to their deadly designs against us. As President Bush said recently, "After all the action we have taken, after all the progress we have made against terror, there is a temptation to think the danger has passed. The danger hasn't passed....America must not forget the lessons of September 11th." Indeed, danger is present in a growing number of places, and we must be vigilant in recognizing—and then confronting—these emerging threats against our common security.

A View from the White House

The White House

The administration of President Barack Obama recognized that, despite the end of the Cold War upon the fall of the Soviet Union, the United States and the other nations of the world had to remain vigilant in preventing nuclear terrorism from joining the ranks of conventional terrorism. Obama first offered an approach in 2009 that he believed would not only keep nuclear weapons out of the hands of unstable leaders and even terrorists but eliminate them altogether. The Nuclear Security Summit was a forum for Obama to express his hope for a nuclear-free future.

The Obama Administration's focus on nuclear security is part of a comprehensive nuclear policy presented by the President in Prague in 2009. In that speech, President Obama described a four-pronged agenda to pursue a world without nuclear weapons. He laid out new U.S. policies and initiatives towards nuclear disarmament, nuclear nonproliferation, nuclear security, and nuclear energy.

President Obama in his Prague remarks identified the risk of nuclear terrorism as the most immediate and extreme threat to global security, and he called for a worldwide effort to secure all vulnerable nuclear materials in four years. He also highlighted the need to break up black markets, detect and intercept materials in transit, and use financial tools to disrupt illicit trade in nuclear materials.

"FACT SHEET: The Nuclear Security Summits: Securing the World from Nuclear Terrorism," The White House, March 29, 2016.

The Nuclear Threat

It is almost impossible to quantify the likelihood of nuclear attack by extremist groups. But we know that roughly 2000 metric tons of nuclear weapons usable materials—highly enriched uranium and separated plutonium—are present in both civilian and military programs, and we know that terrorists have the intent and the capability to turn these materials into a nuclear device if they were to gain access to them. A terrorist attack with an improvised nuclear device would create political, economic, social, psychological, and environmental havoc around the world, no matter where the attack occurs. The threat is global, the impact of a nuclear terrorist attack would be global, and the solutions therefore must be global.

The President's call-to-action in Prague was intended to reinvigorate existing bilateral and multilateral efforts and to challenge nations to re-examine their own commitments to nuclear security. Given the global repercussions of such an attack, all nations have a common interest in establishing the highest levels of security and protection over nuclear material and strengthening national and international efforts to prevent nuclear smuggling and detect and intercept nuclear materials in transit. World leaders have no greater responsibility than ensuring their people and neighboring countries are safe by securing nuclear materials and preventing nuclear terrorism.

Nuclear Security Summit Successes

The Nuclear Security Summit process has been the centerpiece of these efforts. Since the first Summit in April 2010 in Washington, DC, President Obama and more than 50 world leaders have been working together to prevent nuclear terrorism and counter nuclear smuggling. This Summit community has built an impressive track record in meaningful progress towards nuclear security, and on actions that back up our words. Collectively, Summit participants have made over 260 national security commitments in the first three Summits, and of these, over three-quarters have been implemented. In 2016, participants made nearly 90 additional national commitments, not including the additional actions in the 2016 gift baskets and joint statements. These outcomes—nuclear material removed or eliminated, treaties ratified and implemented, reactors converted, regulations strengthened, "Centers of Excellence" launched, technologies upgraded, capabilities enhanced—are tangible, concrete evidence of improved nuclear security. Through its very substantial funding and commitments of expertise and technical resources, the international community has made it harder than ever for terrorists to acquire nuclear weapons, and that has made us all more secure.

In addition to national actions, Summits have provided opportunities for countries to step beyond the limitations of consensus to highlight steps they are actually taking as a group to reduce nuclear threats. These so-called "gift baskets" have reflected joint commitments related to countering nuclear smuggling, mitigating insider threat, radioactive source security, information security, transportation security, and many other topics. This progress would almost certainly not all have transpired in the absence of the kind of high-level forcing effect that summits can have.

Across the four Nuclear Security Summits, we have created and maintained increased momentum of tangible actions to reduce the threat of nuclear terrorism and to make progress towards strengthened international norms and standards for nuclear security.

- The number of facilities with nuclear material continues to decline: We successfully completed removals or confirmed the downblending of highly enriched uranium (HEU) and plutonium from more than 50 facilities in 30 countries—in total, enough material for over 150 nuclear weapons. This work has resulted in the entire continent of South America and wide swaths of central Europe completely free of these dangerous materials. Once Indonesia completes disposal of its HEU, Southeast Asia will join these regions as being free of all such material.

- In 2010, Ukraine committed to remove four bombs' worth of HEU and completed that removal in 2012, fully eliminating all HEU from its territory—a particularly vital step in light of Russia's subsequent breaches of Ukraine's sovereignty and territorial integrity.

- In 2016, Japan removed over 500 kilograms of HEU and separated plutonium from its Fast Critical Assembly. This is the largest project by a country to remove civilian nuclear material from its territory through the Summit process and we look forward to continued work with Japan on converting the Kyoto University Critical Assembly to the use of LEU and removing the HEU fuel.

- Fourteen countries and Taiwan highlighted the elimination of all nuclear materials from their territory; as a result, wide swaths of Central and Eastern Europe and all of South America can be considered free of HEU and therefore no longer targets for those seeking nuclear materials.

- Security at sites and on borders is increasing: All Summit countries reported progress in enhancing nuclear security practices, including 37 countries committing to increase cooperation to counter nuclear smuggling efforts, and 14 countries pledging to improve nuclear detection practices at ports.

- A majority of Summit states will implement stronger security practices: 38 countries, including China and India at the 2016 Summit, pledged to implement stronger nuclear security practices in their countries by—among other things— incorporating international guidelines into national laws, inviting international peer reviews of their nuclear material, and committing to continuous review and improvement of their nuclear security systems.

- The legal basis for nuclear security continues to be strengthened: additional countries are adopting binding legal commitments, such as the Amended Convention on the Physical Protection of Nuclear Material, which will enter into force on May 8, 2016 with over 80 new ratifications since 2009, and the International Convention for the Suppression of Acts of Nuclear Terrorism.

- Nuclear Security Training and Support Centers and other nuclear security Centers of Excellence have increased and become more connected: 15 states have opened centers since 2009 in support of national nuclear workforce training requirements, as well as international capacity building and research and development on nuclear security technologies.

- Radioactive source security has been enhanced: 28 countries agreed to further cooperate on the security and managing the end of life their most dangerous radioactive sources, as well as to explore alternative technology to ultimate replace high activity radioactive sources.

Strengthening the Architecture

Key aspects of the Summits' success have included the personal attention of national leaders; a focus on tangible, meaningful outcomes; a regular event that elicits deliverables and announcements; and a forum that builds relationships that can help advance joint efforts. We need to find ways to capture some of these attributes in more lasting vehicles to promote nuclear security progress.

The IAEA's first-ever nuclear security ministerial held in 2013 is an important step towards strengthening the Agency's role in promoting nuclear security, and we look forward to regularizing those high-level meetings, with the next one being held in December 2016. The 2012 Secretary General's High Level Meeting at the UN on countering nuclear terrorism reflects the unique convening power of the United Nations in this arena. INTERPOL plays a unique role in bringing together law enforcement officials, as seen through its convening of the Global Combat Nuclear Smuggling Conference in January 2016. Other fora for collective action—the Global Partnership, the Global Initiative to Combat Nuclear Terrorism (GICNT), the Nuclear Suppliers Group—have all been invigorated in recent years. The United States hosted the first Nuclear Security

Regulators Conference in 2012, and Spain will host the second such meeting in May 2016 and we look forward to future such conferences. The World Institute for Nuclear Security, professional societies and nongovernmental expert communities are also key components of this architecture and must continue to contribute to this mission as we move beyond Summits to nurture new concepts, build professional skills, and develop global connections.

The Summits were designed to enhance, elevate, expand and empower this architecture of treaties, institutions, norms and practices to effectively address the threats we face today and in the future. As the 2016 Nuclear Security Summit represented the last summit in this format, we have issued five Action Plans in support of the key enduring institutions and initiatives related to nuclear security: the UN, the IAEA, INTERPOL, the GICNT and the Global Partnership. These Action Plans represent steps the Summit participants will take as members of these organizations to support their future development as well as highlight our ambitions for their enhanced role in nuclear security. The activities outlined in these plans will lead to a strengthened global nuclear security architecture poised to address future challenges and threats to security worldwide.

Another key component of the Summit's success has been the effective network of "Sherpas"—the senior expert officials in each Summit country responsible for developing the outcomes of the Summits and for preparing their respective leaders. These Sherpas cut across multiple agencies to form a tight-knit community of action. This community will be carried forward as a "Nuclear Security Contact Group" that will meet regularly to synchronize efforts to implement commitments made in the four Summit Communiqués, national statements, gift baskets, and Action Plans. Recognizing the interest from those who have not been part of the Summit process, this Contact Group will be open to countries that wish to promote the Summit agenda.

Looking Ahead

As much as we have accomplished through the Summit process, more work remains. The IAEA continues to receive reports about nuclear and other radioactive materials found outside regulatory control. We will continue to seek additional tangible results in nuclear material reductions and better overall nuclear and radiological security practices; we will look for ways to enhance the global nuclear security architecture; and, we will continue to promote an architecture that—over time—is comprehensive in its scope (including civilian and military material), is based on international standards, incorporates measures to build confidence that states are applying security responsibly in their countries, and promotes declining stocks of directly usable fissile material.

We all need to do more together to enhance nuclear security performance, to dissuade and apprehend nuclear traffickers, to eliminate excess nuclear weapons and material, to avoid production of materials we cannot use, to make sure our facilities can repel the full range of threats we have already seen in our neighborhoods, to share experiences and best practices, and to do so in ways that are visible to friends, neighbors, and rivals—and thereby provide assurance that we are effectively executing our sovereign responsibility. We also need to reflect the principle of continuous improvement, because nuclear security is never "done." As long as materials exist, they require our utmost commitment to their protection—we continue the march toward the goal of a world without nuclear weapons.

Trump's Nuclear Policy: Too Uninformed or Too Early to Tell?

Zack Beauchamp

Writer Zack Beauchamp, who offered his political views on ThinkProgress and the Dish before writing for Vox, expressed his wonderment and dismay at the words of the future president during the campaign about the arms race. Beauchamp cited the stated desire of Trump to renew the stockpiling of nuclear weapons in what the author believes was the misguided notion of mutually assured destruction during the Cold War. Beauchamp, like many Americans, feared that Trump simply did not know enough about the issue to express them with clarity or—worse yet—deal with them after he had been voted into the Oval Office.

J ust days before his inauguration, Donald Trump made headlines by trashing America's European allies in an interview with two of Europe's biggest newspapers. The hubbub over Trump's attack on Europe obscured one of the stranger comments in the interview— that he hoped to work with Russian strongman Vladimir Putin to reduce both countries' nuclear arsenals.

"Let's see if we can make some good deals with Russia," Trump said. "For one thing, I think nuclear weapons should be way down and reduced very substantially."

To say this is a flip-flop is an understatement. Less than a month ago, Trump tweeted that the US "must greatly strengthen and

"Donald Trump's Very Confusing Thoughts on Nuclear Weapons, Explained," by Zack Beauchamp, Vox Media, Inc., January 18, 2017. Reprinted by Permission. http://www.vox .com/world/2017/1/18/14310168/trump-nuclear-policy-inauguration-explained.

expand its nuclear capability until such time as the world comes to its senses regarding nukes." When MSNBC's Mika Brzezinski asked him about the possibility of this policy setting off an arms race with Russia (which is also talking about expanding/modernizing its nuclear arsenal), Trump's answer was simple.

"Let it be an arms race."

Nuclear arms control is a hugely important issue—especially in a world where tensions between the US and two other nuclear powers, Russia and China, are heating up. So where does Trump stand: with his comments from December, or with his comments from January?

The truth is that nobody knows—leaving us in the dark on one of the very few policy issues with the potential to transform the future of human civilization.

"It's difficult to discern what Trump's policy will be and whether he has given more than a few minutes' thought to these issues," Kingston Reif, the director for disarmament and threat reduction policy at the Arms Control Association, tells me.

The strange history of Trump on nuclear weapons

Questions about nuclear policy have dogged Trump for more than a year now. In a December 2015 Republican debate, moderator Hugh Hewitt asked Trump about the "nuclear triad"—America's three-part system for delivering nuclear weapons (bombers, submarines, and intercontinental ballistic missiles). Trump's answer was confusing:

> We have to be extremely vigilant and extremely careful when it comes to nuclear. Nuclear changes the whole ballgame. ... The biggest problem we have is nuclear—nuclear proliferation and having some maniac, having some madman go out and get a nuclear weapon. That's in my opinion, that is the single biggest problem that our country faces right now.

There are two interesting things about this. First, Trump suggests, as he later did in his January interview, that he sees large global nuclear stockpiles as a problem. Second, he doesn't appear to know any of the major policy questions surrounding the nuclear triad, or even what the nuclear triad is.

That became especially clear when Hewitt followed up, pressing Trump to answer the actual question about the triad. Trump's response? "I think—I think, for me, nuclear is just the power, the devastation is very important to me."

This pattern—an abstract abhorrence of nuclear weapons but seemingly confused views on actual nuclear policy—continued throughout the campaign. In a March 2016 town hall, for example, host Chris Matthews pressed Trump on whether he'd use nuclear weapons. He seemed to say both no and yes at the same time, saying he'd be "the last one to use nuclear weapons," but also that he would be very willing to nuke ISIS territory in response to a terrorist attack:

> TRUMP: I'd be the last one to use the nuclear weapons, because that's sort of like the end of the ballgame.
>
> MATTHEWS: So, can you take it off the table now? Can you tell the Middle East we are not using the nuclear weapon on anybody?
>
> TRUMP: I would never say that. I would never take any of my cards off the table...
>
> MATTHEWS: Where would we drop—where would we drop a nuclear weapon in the Middle East?
>
> TRUMP: Let me explain. Let me explain. Somebody hits us within ISIS—you wouldn't fight back with a nuke?

In August, MSNBC host Joe Scarborough recounted a story an unnamed foreign policy expert told him about Trump and nukes. In it, Trump expresses confusion as to why the US doesn't use its nukes.

"Several months ago, a foreign policy expert on the international level went to advise Donald Trump. And three times [Trump] asked about the use of nuclear weapons. Three times he asked at one point if we had them why can't we use them," Scarborough said.

During the first general election debate, in September 2016, moderator Lester Holt asked a more specific version of Matthews's question—what Trump thought about a "no first use" policy. That's the idea that the US should swear off launching a nuclear strike against an enemy unless it has been attacked with nukes first.

Here was Trump's answer:

Russia has been expanding their—they have a much newer capability than we do. We have not been updating from the new standpoint. I looked the other night. I was seeing B-52s, they're old enough that your father, your grandfather could be flying them. We are not—we are not keeping up with other countries.

I would like everybody to end it, just get rid of it. But I would certainly not do first strike. I think that once the nuclear alternative happens, it's over. At the same time, we have to be prepared. I can't take anything off the table.

Trump's answer, once again, gestures at hating nuclear weapons ("just get rid of it"). But he also implies that he supports developing more advanced ways of delivering nuclear weapons—which the US is already doing.

But when it came to Holt's actual question, about his views on no first use as a policy, Trump had no real answer. He's said both, "I would certainly not do first strike," *and,* "I can't take anything off the table"—but those are opposite things. The whole point of a no-first-strike policy is taking a first strike off the table. That means Trump literally had never heard of the no-first-use debate, had never thought about it enough to have an actual opinion, or didn't for some reason want to say what that opinion was.

By the time Trump won the election, experts on nuclear policy were thoroughly confused. There was simply no consistent policy throughline, no meaningful ability to figure out what Trump truly plans to do with the only weapons that have the power to destroy the Earth in minutes.

"To journalists asking me what nuclear policies Trump will adopt: I have absolutely no idea," James Acton, the director of the Carnegie Endowment for International Peace's Nuclear Policy Program, wrote two days after Trump's upset win. "And neither, I strongly suspect, does he."

Trump's actual nuclear policy has not gotten clearer

If you squint at this history of Trump comments, you can kind of put together a consistent line.

It seems that Trump thinks nuclear weapons are extremely dangerous and that the world should work on eliminating them. But in the absence of any agreements to do so, the United States should maintain and even expand its nuclear arsenal to make sure it's deadlier than that of any peer competitor.

Read in this light, there's *some* consistency between Trump's December and January lines. In December, he was expressing what the US should do absent arms control agreement—expand and upgrade its nuclear stockpile. In January, by contrast, he was expressing his support for an agreement between the US and Russia that might make this unnecessary.

These views have some foundation in real policy problems. As my colleague Yochi Dreazen explains, there's a widespread worry in the national security community that America's system for delivering nukes is starting to show cracks—to take one high-profile example, an investigation found that missileers at one base in Montana were routinely cheating on their proficiency exams, meaning they might not actually be able to launch. Failures like this, and the need to make sure nukes actually function, has led the Obama administration to devote about $1 trillion over the next 30 years to nuclear maintenance and growth.

You can support modernizing America's remaining nukes and, at the same time, work to reduce the overall number of nukes the United States has. This is what the Obama administration has done, concluding a treaty with Russia—called New START—to cut the overall number of weapons possessed by both countries. Trump pursuing this would be welcome news to the nuclear policy community—current stockpiles are easily large enough to extinguish all life on Earth. If Trump did strike a bargain with Putin that builds on New START, that would count as a real accomplishment for his unprecedented policy of buddying up to the Kremlin.

Stop Trump from Starting a New Nuclear Arms Race

Before the Election, Donald Trump reportedly asked CIA briefers "If we have nuclear weapons, why can't we use them?" He also suggested that Japan, South Korea, and even Saudi Arabia should obtain their own nuclear weapons. He demonstrated no awareness or respect for the decades of bipartisan consensus for reducing and stopping the spread of nuclear weapons.

These were clear signs of an impulsive and reckless approach to the most sobering and awesome Presidential power of all: being able to single-handedly order the use of US nuclear weapons. Even before he gets that power, President-Elect Trump impetuously tweeted a threat to resume the nuclear arms race, wasting trillions of taxpayer dollars and recklessly imperiling the survival of humanity anew.

Mr. Trump is dramatically increasing the risk that accidents or miscalculation in the wake of this horrifying and unprecedented "anti-diplomacy through tweets" could cause a nuclear holocaust, hardly something US voters supported in the November 8 Election. A recent highly reputable study revealed that the use of even 100 of the 15,500 nuclear weapons remaining could cause two billion deaths—nearly one of every three people now living.

[...]

When the administration of former President Ronald Reagan recklessly talked of nuclear warning shots, and of fighting and "winning" a nuclear war, a massive citizen movement fought back and forced President Reagan to resume nuclear arms negotiations. Those led to the first nuclear reduction treaty in history in 1987.

Subsequently, Republican Presidents George H. W. Bush, and George W. Bush took steps to further reduce nuclear weapons, and Democratic Presidents Bill Clinton and Barack Obama acted similarly. The world's nuclear arsenals have been reduced by over 75% as a result of this bipartisan policy of reducing the nuclear threat through verifiable agreements and initiatives.

[...]

—"Stop **Trump from Starting a New Nuclear Arms Race!**" by Coalition for Peace Action, December 30, 2016.

But the issue is that it is very hard to figure out what Trump's inchoate feelings mean in terms of actual policies like these. His comments on nukes are so vague, and so abstract, that it's very difficult to understand how they translate in concrete policy terms.

Does Trump now support a no-first-use doctrine? Does he support entirely eliminating nuclear weapons, a goal known as "global zero," or merely further reductions in the US and Russian stockpiles? Would he keep New START in place? What about the Anti-Ballistic Missile Treaty or the Comprehensive Test Ban Treaty, two major nuclear policy agreements?

On these points—again, the stuff that actually matters—Trump is radically unclear.

"Until we can see what exactly is on the table and what the possible outcomes might be, we will withhold judgment on Mr. Trump's proposal," Reif says. "The devil is always in the details."

You can see this policy incoherence on a closer examination of the December and January comments. Remember, Trump didn't just say in December that he'd be fine with the US modernizing its nukes—he said he'd be fine with an *out-and-out arms race*. If nuclear stockpiles are so dangerous, as Trump has suggested he believes, then it seems like he'd want to avoid something that would lead to their rapid growth.

But he doesn't, really. Trump has vague, abstract feelings about nuclear weapons, but nothing in his public comments suggests he has any real sense of how those feelings translate into actual policy.

"This week it's reductions; last week it's an arms race," Acton tweeted. "Don't treat these utterances as serious policy statements."

Other policy experts agree.

"Unhappily, there's not much substance here on arms reductions," Joshua Pollack, a senior research associate at Middlebury's James Martin Center for Nonproliferation Studies, wrote earlier this week.

"Sanctions should persuade behavior shift on Ukraine, Syria & hacking. This [nuclear negotiation proposal] seems like desperate pretense for lifting," Ben Loehrke, the policy program officer for nuclear security at the Stanley Foundation, tweeted around the same time.

Now, Trump's national security team has at least one member who knows about nukes. Defense secretary nominee James Mattis, a retired Marine general, was asked repeatedly about nuclear weapons. Unsurprisingly, he demonstrated real familiarity with nuclear policy issues—making clear that he sees nukes as a deterrent and is deeply hostile to their use, implying opposition to the creation of a drone that could drop nuclear bombs, supporting modernizing all three legs of the triad, and the like.

"We must continue with current nuclear modernization plans for all three legs of the triad, and for associated command and control systems," Mattis said. "What we're trying to do is set such a stance with our triad that these weapons must never be used."

But Mattis isn't actually going to be in charge of nuclear weapons. That's under the Department of Energy's purview, a division of labor that has its origins in Harry Truman's desire to keep the nuclear stockpile under civilian control. Trump's nominee to lead the Department of Energy, former Texas Gov. Rick Perry, has demonstrated no meaningful knowledge of nuclear weapons. He once supported abolishing the Energy Department entirely.

Ultimately, then, we're in the dark about how the Trump administration will handle nukes—no closer to understanding Trump's nuclear policy than we were the day he was elected.

VIEWPOINT 5

President Trump Versus North Korea—a Nuclear Catastrophe

James Johnson

Preelection fears about foreign policy and nuclear threats under President Trump came true when, in 2017, tensions skyrocketed between the US and North Korea. In the following viewpoint, politics and international relations expert James Johnson, who holds a PhD from the University of Leicester, warns that North Korea's missile tests and the president's incendiary remarks make for an explosive combination that could very well lead to nuclear war or, at the very least, "a permanent state of crisis."

According to a US Defense Intelligence Agency report, Pyongyang's nuclear capabilities and conventional long range missile programmes are gathering momentum at a rapid clip. The report indicated that North Korea has successfully manufactured a miniaturised nuclear warhead that can fit onto its ballistic missiles, including intercontinental ballistic missiles (ICBMs). The report added that the reclusive state has as many as 60 nuclear weapons, well surpassing previous estimates.

Despite the missile tests, there's plenty of scepticism over whether or not North Korea has developed the re-entry vehicle technology needed to land a warhead. Still, the country's nuclear strike capability has probably crossed a point of no return: it has developed the ability to deliver a nuclear warhead to continental US.

Donald Trump famously asserted that he would not allow Pyongyang to develop nuclear weapons capable of reaching US soil; in this he and his predecessors have clearly failed. The exchange of threats and provocative sabre rattling on both sides suggests that the possibility of miscalculation, miscommunication, deterrence failure, and state of crisis in East Asia has become an increasingly dangerous geostrategic reality—neither side appears prepared to back down from their diplomatic one-upmanship.

Over the past few weeks, the incendiary and escalatory barbs from Washington and Pyongyang have escalated. Trump thundered that Pyongyang's threats "will be met with fire and fury like the world has never seen"; Pyongyang said it was planning an attack on US bases at Guam. Trump then upped the ante, telling reporters that his "fire and fury" comments were not tough enough and that Kim Jong-un would "truly regret" any threats to the US or its allies. He also said that US military capabilities were "locked and loaded" in case North Korea "acted unwisely."

This all implies that the US could countenance a nuclear first strike. But Trump hasn't clarified precisely what would constitute an "unwise" action, nor what Kim Jong-un would have to do to prevent an American attack. This bellicose but vague rhetoric has caused anxiety in the Asia-Pacific, with some governments (especially China) urging restraint.

The bottom line, however is clear: Washington has very few viable options, and the potential for a serious nuclear crisis could be just a few words (or tweets) away. So how likely is war, and can it be stopped?

Polarised and tense

The short answer is that in the best case scenario, the US should brace itself for a permanent state of crisis or Cold War. Inadvertently or otherwise, Trump has painted himself into a strategic corner.

The North Korean problem is highly complex. All parties involved—the US, Japan, South Korea, China, and Russia—will have to be part of any solution, and Washington is pressuring Beijing in particular to lean harder on Kim. But ultimately, Pyongyang's top security objectives (achieve international recognition as a nuclear armed state) are diametrically opposed to Washington's (denuclearise the Korean Peninsula), leaving almost no space for compromise or non-military solutions.

Much of this was true before the latest war of words, but thanks to Trump, the whole deterrence calculus has changed. Pyongyang has long understood that it would only incur the US's nuclear "fire and fury" by itself using nuclear weapons first. But Trump's recent statements suggest that if the Kim government threatens the US or its allies, he might actually contemplate a preventative nuclear strike.

History has shown that brinkmanship can rapidly escalate. States' attempts to signal resolve and strength can lead to misperception and miscalculation, and any minor incident (for example, a naval skirmish or aircraft collision) on the Korean peninsula could rapidly escalate to a nuclear strike. If this were to happen, the chain of events would likely be beyond the control of either Trump or Kim.

Is Trump bluffing?

Worryingly, there is no shortage of hawks in Washington urging the administration to launch a preventive attack. Analysts have drawn parallels with Trump's rhetoric and the "rain of ruin speech" that then president Truman delivered in 1945 after ordering the use of a nuclear bomb on Hiroshima. To be sure, Trump's rhetoric has eclipsed even the harshest language previous US administrations have used to warn Pyongyang off any further provocations.

In international relations, words matter, especially when nuclear weapons are involved. And whether or not Trump is prepared to back up what he says with action, when US presidents speak, other leaders listen. If he has no intention of carrying out his threat in the face of Pyongyang's provocations, the strategic consequences could be huge.

A bluff exposed would gravely undermine the nuclear deterrence the US offers to its allies, and in turn embolden Pyongyang's nuclear weapons programme and strengthen Kim's hand as he tries to disrupt South Korea and Japan's relationship with the US's security architecture. Those two countries might also explore ways to substitute America's extended nuclear deterrence with their own nuclear weapons—guaranteeing permanent enmity from China and Russia.

Whether Trump's shoot-from-the-hip loose words are merely a negotiating ploy or part of a carefully calibrated stratagem to deter Kim, they are unlikely to work. Trump's erratic style has drawn comparisons with Nixon's so-called madman theory: coercing an adversary into negotiations by signalling the US president is sufficiently unhinged to carry out a catastrophic attack.

But whereas Nixon relied on clear messages and military signals, the Trump administration's unpredictability and mixed messages suggest impulsiveness, not strategic coherence. This tactic risks fuelling Pyongyang's fear for the survival of the regime to the point where it might contemplate a desperate and suicidal last stand, nuclear or otherwise.

The bottom line is that regardless of how seriously threats are intended, rhetorical escalation is dangerous. You don't bluff—and you certainly don't bluff and then back down.

VIEWPOINTS ON
MODERN WORLD HISTORY

CHAPTER 3

Planning a Peaceful Future

Preface

T he poignant warning of George Santayana aside, history can only teach so much. What has passed only brings limited clarity to the future. World leaders and concerned citizens must now search for solutions to what remains a potentially catastrophic nuclear threat. What has and has not worked previously can be used as a measuring stick, but many believe that only bold new initiatives can ensure that the planet will be saved from destruction.

Such daring plans, however, can only be achieved if world leaders are open to them. And that means prudent solutions to current problems—such as the growing nuclear threat from rogue nations—before the nations of the world can embark on any new paths to global security. The final chapter of this book will mix the practicality needed to deal with current issues with idealistic dreams of the future. Only an open-minded outlook from the nations of the globe can transform those dreams into reality.

The opinions of several experts in the field are featured here. They express views that indeed extend from the very practical to the very idealistic. They ask and seek to answer questions involving the realistic potential of foolproof missile defense systems and preventing nations from upgrading their nuclear arsenals. They also ask and seek to answer questions involving the possibility of global nuclear disarmament and a world government, both of which could, for all intents and purposes, solve the problem.

One drawback of futuristic thinking is that it does not always take into account surprises on the global stage. One could not, for instance, have predicted the renewal of hostilities between the United States and Russia during the reigns of Barack Obama and Vladimir Putin, which again raised the specter of a runaway arms race. Or the undaunted push by North Korean leader Kim Jong-un to gain nuclear capability and threaten with nuclear war the United States and other nations that had the audacity to seek an end to what most considered to be his madness. Or the diplomatic deal with Iran that many believe has ended its nuclear threat and others claim it has done nothing of the sort and has only emboldened it.

Can bold and idealistic initiatives solve such problems throughout the world or must the problems be solved first through practical solutions before such daring and creative plans be undertaken? Nobody knows for sure. The only thing everybody does understand is that nuclear proliferation must he addressed and defeated if the people of the world are to live without fear of utter extinction.

Getting MAD to Go Away

The Association for Diplomatic Studies and Training

Though the Strategic Defense Initiative espoused by President Reagan in 1983 has been for the most part rejected as science fiction, its motivation as a rejection of the theory of mutually assured destruction (MAD) has resulted in a more positive and realistic outlook in regard to solving the problem of nuclear proliferation. The following viewpoint from the ADST, an independent, nonprofit organization located at the State Department's George P. Shultz National Foreign Affairs Training Center, looks at the circumstances and history surrounding "Star Wars" and how it relates to the battles being fought today. A number of experts in the field were interviewed as the reader is transported back to the early 1980s and what was the last decade of the Cold War.

O n March 23rd, 1983, President Ronald Reagan announced the Strategic Defense Initiative, signaling a massive paradigm shift in U.S. policy on nuclear policy. Dubbed "Star Wars" after the 1977 movie, SDI represented Reagan's rejection of Mutual Assured Destruction. MAD had fostered an uneasy peace during the Cold War as neither the U.S. nor the USSR attacked the other knowing that it would in turn be the target of a massive nuclear retaliation annihilating it (and much of the planet). By extension, so the argument went, a weapons system that could deflect most of an opponent's nuclear barrage would undermine MAD by making

"Moments in U.S. Diplomatic History," drawn from the Foreign Affairs Oral History Collection of the Association for Diplomatic Studies and Training, Arlington, Virginia, http://www.adst.org/moments.

that country feel more protected and thus potentially more likely to at least consider launching an offensive attack.

For that reason, many in U.S. government, including high-ranking officials at the State and Defense Departments, did not support SDI; they were also not consulted before the surprise announcement. As designed, SDI would use space-based lasers, particle beams, satellites, and other "space-age" weapons, in contravention of the Treaty on Outer Space, to shoot down ballistic missiles before they reached their targets. Given its utter complexity and reliance on unproven technology, SDI was viewed by many as unrealistic. Nevertheless, the announcement sent shock waves throughout the world.

This account was compiled from interviews done by Charles Stuart Kennedy with: James W. Chamberlin in 1997, a Special Assistant in Space Matter for the Arms Control and Disarmament Agency (ACDA); Aloysius M. O'Neill in 2008, a member of the State Department's Office of Strategic Technology Affairs; Philip Merrill in 1997, a Defense Department Counselor; Ambassador Thomas M. T. Niles in 1998, the Deputy Assistant Secretary for European Affairs; Roger G. Harrison in 2001, the Political-Military Counselor in London.

Craig Dunkerley, who handled NATO issues in the State Department's European Affairs Bureau, was interviewed in 2004; Secretary of Defense Frank Carlucci was interviewed in 1997; Dr. William Lloyd Stearman, a member of the National Security Council, in 1992; and Ambassador Rudolph V. Perina, a political officer at the U.S. Mission NATO in Brussels, interviewed in 2006. Also used is the account of Ambassador Maynard Wayne Glitman, Deputy Negotiator on the INF (Intermediate-Range Nuclear Forces) Treaty negotiations, who was interviewed by James S. Pacy in 2001.

CHAMBERLIN: Star Wars, SDI, or the Strategic Defense Initiative was intended to defend the U.S. from missile attack, particularly from the Soviet Union. It envisaged a very sophisticated system that would stop thousands of missiles within only a few minutes after launch, detection and warning. It was a clear violation of the anti-ballistic missile (ABM) treaty. It was the bane of my existence…. It was a serious threat to the ABM treaty, as well as the Treaty on the Peaceful Uses of Outer Space.

MERRILL: I remember watching a nationally televised Presidential speech….Tacked on to the end, and totally unconnected to the rest of the remarks, were ten minutes of argument proposing a national program to research and develop defensive technologies. All of us were surprised but also pleased because at long last the grip of MAD [mutual assured destruction] on the nation's nuclear posture had been opened if not broken. The next day the *New York Post* headline read "Star Wars to Zap Red Nukes." Star Wars it became.

Q: There was no consultation within the government on this issue?.

NILES: There certainly wasn't. SDI was based on President Reagan's very deep aversion to nuclear weapons and to the MAD doctrine. You saw it again in October 1986 at the Reykjavik Summit with President Gorbachev during which President Reagan advanced the idea of the total elimination of nuclear weapons, which Gorbachev accepted. The stumbling block then was President Reagan's insistence that SDI continue.

In 1983, as today, missile defense, whether it is SDI or some other program, was based on a confluence of two philosophical views: 1) an aversion to nuclear weapons; and 2) a theological hostility to arms control, which focuses on the 1972 ABM Treaty.

President Reagan was motivated by his aversion to nuclear weapons, and the people at the top of the Department of Defense—civilians, not uniformed military—who were responsible for the details of SDI, to the extent there were any, were motivated by their ideological hatred of arms control and the ABM Treaty. As far as I know, the State Department was out of the picture.

Keep in mind that, at least in theory, SDI represented a fundamental shift in United States defense policy, taken without consultations with our Allies. Although ultimately we were able to work things out with the Europeans on SDI, so that they were able to participate in some development contracts, the damage was never fully overcome.

At the beginning, the Europeans saw SDI as a serious threat to NATO itself because if, hypothetically, the United States were able to achieve a security system that would protect us against Soviet ballistic missiles, what did this say about our nuclear guarantee for Europe, which at least in theory was designed to protect them against the overwhelming Soviet preponderance in armored forces in Central Europe?

The Europeans saw SDI as an indication that the United States, at least theoretically, was interested in backing away from this commitment to Europe and building a "Fortress America," with this high-tech system that would protect us, but not them.

The proposal was seen in Europe as changing American nuclear policy without consulting the Allies with whom the policy had been developed. It was a real bombshell. The "evil empire" speech to the religious broadcasters, which came a week or 10 days before the SDI announcement, was likewise seen as a sign of something strange going on in the United States, not that the Europeans thought that the Soviet Union was a nice place, or that the Soviet leaders were nice guys. But, the using the term "evil empire" in public struck them—even [British Primer Minister] Mrs. Thatcher—as being a little heavy.

[The Reagan announcement] was a total surprise to everyone working on the issue, at least at my level. I had had some inklings from NSC [National Security Council] staff that they wanted to keep their options open, but I don't know if they knew about SDI or were just reflecting a general Republican policy that opposed space arms control. Some senior officials may have known before Reagan's speech, but the people in the bureaucracy were all surprised. Certainly in ACDA [Arms Control and Disarmament Agency], most people were upset about it; that is an understatement—they were outraged.

HARRISON: The Star Wars speech [took] our bureaucracy and theirs by surprise, and it changed 35 years of nuclear strategy overnight. It showed the power of a popular president who knows what he knows. A lobby group called High Frontier had produced this cartoon of laser platforms in space destroying nuclear warheads. It looked like a good idea. Complete fantasy at the time, and a complete fantasy now as far as that goes. It had great political appeal and Reagan was a great politician, maybe the best certainly since FDR, a man who knew what would appeal. If it appealed to him, it would appeal to the electorate, and it did.

But it didn't appeal to the people who had laboring in the vineyards for years to build or limit weapons in keeping with existing nuclear strategy, and now found their assumptions— particularly the assumption that defensive measures were really offensive in effect, since they would prevent retaliation and therefore encourage preemption—overthrown. Defense, in short, would invalidate mutual assured destruction. MAD was all bloodthirsty, awful, academic nonsense of course, but Reagan was the first President to question it. MAD just didn't make sense to him.

DUNKERLEY: SDI became a major issue because it constituted a new and potentially significant direction for U.S. defense policy—one with implications not just for the relationship with our strategic adversary of that time, the Soviet Union, but no less for the fundamentals of our security relationships with allies and friends in the context of deterrence.

That is to say, how might SDI impact perceptions of stability, or instability, within a structure of mutual assured deterrence that had grown up with our primary adversary? How might SDI come to affect hard-won political and military credibility of the structure of extended deterrence that had been built up at the core of NATO strategy over the years? Those were tough questions.

The concept of SDI at that most initial stage was at a high level of abstraction with considerable political symbolism and many practical uncertainties. Therefore one of the immediate tasks, at least from the perspective of those working such issues at State, was to develop a better sense of its potential substance and strategic direction in the face of a host of immediate questions and anxieties on the part of the Allies let alone the Soviets. Within the EUR [European Affairs] Bureau at least, we spent a good deal of time during this period, both in interagency debate and consultation with the allies, seeking to explore what SDI could come to represent in the context of Alliance strategy and to build support for the notion of constructive cooperation in that direction.

At the same time, both Secretary [of State George] Shultz and President Reagan had been sending out signals, even well before Gorbachev's rise, that indicated a readiness, should there be a Soviet return to the nuclear negotiations, to explore a more potentially positive course on a broad, multi-faceted agenda of issues with Moscow. The prospect of SDI, and the prohibitive cost of racing the Americans in this field, seemed to have captured Russian attention and was seen by some as a further factor affecting their decision to return.

But what my EUR colleagues and I did not at that time fully appreciate was the extent to which Soviet internal economic and political problems were mounting, let alone what Gorbachev's advent as a new leader might eventually come to foreshadow in terms of new policies.

CARLUCCI: Gorbachev caught the President by surprise [at the bilateral summit in Reykjavik] and proposed the virtual elimination of nuclear weapons if the President would give up SDI, what the press liked to label Star Wars—a misnomer. At any rate, the administration came very close to agreeing to that but Ronald

Reagan fortunately was unwilling to give up SDI. Obviously, this had a real traumatic effect in Europe.

One of the ceaseless tasks that I had, and my predecessors all had, was trying to convince Ronald Reagan that nuclear weapons were essential to keep the balance between the big powers. The Soviets had conventional superiority and nuclear weapons had actually kept the peace for many years. While we should reduce them—no question we should negotiate a balanced reduction, I was very much in favor of that—to simply eliminate them would put us at very high risk and traumatize our allies.

Of course this was the position Margaret Thatcher took as well. That was very helpful. Ronald Reagan had always been very much against nuclear weapons and the faster you could get rid of them, the better he liked it.

HARRISON: The right wing in Washington had welcomed it because they thought it would make any negotiation with the Soviets impossible. The Soviets would see missile defense as threatening, since it could lessen their retaliatory capability and therefore encourage a U.S. first strike. That's what the doctrine said, and that's what we had argued when the Soviets had dabbled in anti-missile development.

But if Reagan knew about that doctrine, he didn't care about it. The problem was that when you came to negotiating details of an agreement which affected the fate of a thousand or so nuclear warheads, that's serious business, you have to get the details right. The last thing anyone wanted to do was to ask Reagan about details.

Theoretically, the substance of such important agreements had to be a presidential decision, but in practical terms everyone labored long and hard to keep that from being the case. As I said, Defense didn't want these issues to go to Reagan because they were afraid of Reagan's anti-nuclear leanings.

That had been underlined the Reykjavik summit, where Reagan and Gorbachev had agreed, very briefly, to abolish all land-based ICBMs before Reagan could be hauled into a bathroom during a break by Bob Linhard and Richard Perle and told it was impractical thing to do, especially at a time when the Administration was trying to convince Congress to fund a new generation of land-based missiles, the MX.

But Reagan still might have bought the deal, in my opinion, if Gorbachev had not insisted that it be tied to limitations on Reagan's anti-missile program.

STEARMAN: I felt it was smart to develop [SDI] because the Soviets had, in any case, been working on it. I never believed in "mutual assured destruction" and neither did the Soviets. We knew that. I thought it was infinitely preferable to have something that would make our deterrent more credible. This would have contributed greatly to world peace and stability. I was a firm believer without knowing much about the technicalities, but I knew our capabilities and those of the Soviets; so I was confident we could do something.

The problem was that people in this country thought that Reagan had said that we could deploy a leakproof umbrella which would protect us from all missiles. Reagan never really meant that, but, unfortunately, he never said clearly enough that this was not what he had in mind and that 100 percent protection was impossible. It was never explained the way it should have been, I think. So I partly blame Reagan and others in the White House for the widespread skepticism and opposition to SDI.

In a very revealing and generally overlooked interview published in *Time* magazine in early September, 1985, Gorbachev called upon Congress to withhold SDI funding in order to confine it permanently to the laboratory. I couldn't believe that nobody picked up on this. I did, however, in a memo which went to the President.

Nobody else seemed to appreciate the incredible candor of this man. It was of enormous importance to him to continue this détente. It wasn't entirely, of course, just to encourage us not to fund SDI. He also wanted to modernize the Soviet Union and bring it into the later part of the 20th century. There were multiple reasons for his détente and liberalization programs both in foreign policy and domestic policy, but the main objective was killing SDI. I got this indirectly from Gorbachev himself and certainly from a number of other top Soviet leaders who said that SDI was overwhelmingly the factor that led Gorbachev to do what he did… what he felt compelled to do.

So in the summer of 1989, he clearly stated to the Eastern European countries that the Soviet Union would not use force to correct any "mistakes" they made. Referring to Sinatra's song… "Doing it my way," is how the Soviet spokesman explained it at the time.

Q: How did your British colleagues react? How were they seeing this?

HARRISON: Very negatively. They thought it was terrible because, among other things, it was going to end the strategic arms reduction negotiations. MAD was the thing. Our force posture was based on it, the negotiations were based on it, everything was based on it. Although the Soviets never accepted MAD as such, their force posture was based on it, too. As for the British, they were just then trying to get their submarine-based nuclear force modernized— there was great opposition in Parliament—and Reagan was saying, in effect, that we would make nuclear missiles obsolete.

There was also the implication in Reagan's approach, at least from Europe's prospective, that we planned to shelter behind our nuclear defenses and avoid the irritation of dealing with pesky foreigners, including them. I dutifully reported all this negative reaction—it was the FCO [Foreign and Commonwealth Office] reaction, by the way, not so much the public reaction.

Rick Burt, who was then Assistant Secretary for European Affairs, asked for as much negative reaction as we could report. He was a traditional MAD kind of guy, and shared some of the

European view. Jim Dobbins told me that Reagan would probably forget the whole thing in a couple of weeks. Needless to say, he didn't.

The problem for me was that I went on reporting the negative feedback after the political winds in Washington shifted and Burt decided he better get with the program. SDI might contradict three decades of deterrence theory, but he either didn't know or didn't care, which was precisely the right attitude to take, although I didn't think so at the time.

PERINA: My overwhelming impression from NATO was that this was basically a U.S.-run organization. One could really sense that. Most of the Allies were quite deferential to the United States, the French always being a certain exception. In fact, most of the delegates at NATO tended to be even more pro-American than their governments, or at least they tried to give us that impression.

In my time, we never had a really heated discussion at NATO, even though I think many Allies were skeptical of some of our policies such as INF [Intermediate-Range Nuclear Force] deployment and SDI... NATO was a club and largely our club. It was a very friendly environment for the U.S.

CARLUCCI: Gorbachev, as was well known, hated SDI. Not without reason, because he knew it would force a reconfiguration of the Soviet strategic forces. He believed we could do it, unlike a lot of people in the United States. At one point in the deliberations on INF, he said something to George [Shultz] like, "You're going to have to get rid of the SDI."

George, I guess, had been tired of hearing this, and he said, "SDI is really President Reagan's initiative so I'm going to ask Frank [Carlucci] to respond to that."

I was tired of it, too. I guess we were all tired. I said, "Well, Mr. Secretary General, [of the Communist Party] (which is what he was at the time), what you just said is totally unacceptable to the President." With that Gorbachev threw down his pencil. His staff later told me this was not planned—he threw his pencil and said, "If that's the attitude you have, then there won't be a summit."

STEARMAN: One of their principal objectives was to thwart SDI and also to get us to throttle back on the substantial military buildup that Reagan had introduced when he came into office... One thing you have to bear in mind about SDI, which is very important, was that, although it was pooh-poohed in this country by many and not even taken that seriously by some in the NSC, it was taken very seriously in the Soviet Union.

The Soviets had been working on this problem for 30 years, and they were convinced that with our technology and engineering skills that we could do it. If we could come up with a SDI, which was only 50 percent effective, that would radically change the strategic balance in our favor. In fact, we learned that some of their top military leaders believed it could be as much as 65 percent effective.

So from Gorbachev on down, they all believed that we could eventually deploy a strategic defense that would absolutely turn things upside down. One must always bear in mind that military power to the Soviet Union was essentially a political instrument. This seems to be awfully hard for us Americans to understand. The [Soviets] looked upon it as a political and diplomatic tool. I do not believe they ever seriously considered attacking the United States; they certainly never wanted war with us, but they built up their military power in order to gain political and diplomatic leverage.

So they felt that if we gained an enormous strategic advantage over them, they would lose most of the political and diplomatic leverage that their very costly military power had bought them, which was the only thing that made them a superpower. Anyway, they thought SDI was enormously important.

I have subsequently found out that everybody from Gorbachev on down believed it could work. Several years ago, I was sitting next to a Soviet Lt. General at a dinner party and I said, "General, do you people think SDI can work?"

He looked at me as if I had asked him if the sun will come up tomorrow. He said, "Of course." That was a given.

SHOSTAL: I saw a fundamental contradiction in the Soviet response to SDI. On the one hand they would argue that it couldn't work. I remember going to a lecture by a very prominent Soviet physicist, Roald Sagdoyev, in which he said at the University of Hamburg that SDI would never work. That was part one of his presentation.

Part two of his presentation was how this was destabilizing to the relationship between the United States and the Soviet Union and would lead to political tensions. When I heard that it seemed to me that something is strange here and there certainly was a contradiction.

That sense of contradiction converted me from having been initially very critical of SDI, to recognizing that the Soviets were worried about it for other reasons that they really weren't stating. I think those reasons had much to do with the pressure and challenge that SDI represented to their economic system, to their scientific establishment and their fear that they simply wouldn't be able to keep up with American technology development that might result from the SDI.

Q: In foreign affairs the whole Star Wars thing as it developed was really considered to be one of the weights that helped to break the Soviet Union. The technology was such that the Soviets were becoming more and more aware that they couldn't keep pace if we were going to get in to this. Is it true there wasn't much behind it except a thought?

MERRILL: There was much more behind it than most realized, but perhaps not as much as some others thought. What Richard Perle and I both believe is that the Russians thought the U.S. had found a specific route to workable missile defenses. They realized that such a defense was possible even as we did. All we had found, however, was an approach.

The Soviets were ahead of us in understanding there was a revolution in military affairs taking place based on information technology. Point it here; shoot it there. GPS, space based navigation, precision guided missiles. The three great military revolutions taking place in the world involve precision guided weapons, defensive technologies, and transparency of all large objects and fixed sites.

The importance of Star Wars, that is, the SDI program cannot be overstated. If nothing else it convinced the Soviets that we had somehow found the road map to the new information technologies and to what we now call the revolution in military affairs. Whether we had at that time or not is secondary to the point that the Soviets believed we had. It helped make them think they could not compete with us.

Q: I recall that at one point Reagan made a proposal to share the technology with the Soviets so that we could each stop the other's missiles.

PERINA: Right. But the Soviets were convinced it was a trick. They could not believe that we would really share such technology with them, since they would never share it with us if tables were turned.

You have to put this in the context of the revolution that was taking place in the United States and in the West, with average people starting to acquire personal computers, and kids growing up at home and in school with computer skills. The Soviets saw all this, and they were terrified. Their own kids were still working with an abacus in most of their schools.

They saw themselves falling behind technologically in a way that would be qualitative and devastating. They never expressed it that way but one could sense it in talks with them. I was not an expert on SDI. I didn't know if it would or would not work. But I saw it as a useful ploy to motivate the Soviets to change to a freer, more open system that could keep pace with Western technological development.

Their closed, authoritarian system just could not do that. In conversations, they always tried to pick up on Western skepticism and say, "SDI won't work and even your own experts say it won't work."

But I would answer something like "Well, you know, if you can build a missile that can fly 5000 miles and hit a square block, don't you think it would be easier to find some way to throw that missile off course?" They were very scared that this was indeed true and we would beat them to doing it.

The INF and SDI

GLITMAN: In a speech, Gorbachev seemed to put linkage back into effect. In other words, he referred to the settlement of the SDI question as a precondition for moving ahead on his proposal on eliminating all offensive nuclear weapons by the year 2000. The specific linkage with SDI was contained in a sweeping proposal dealing with nuclear arms, which can reach each other's territories, that is strategic arms.

A separate portion of the speech called for the complete liquidation of Soviet and U.S. medium range missiles in the European zone. Again, this is a zero coming out from their side, but limited to the European zone, and as we've seen, the Soviet SS-20s outside of Europe were still capable of hitting targets in most of NATO Europe.

PERINA: The talks never got very far. The Soviets could not stop either SDI or INF deployment. The major obstacle to INF was Western European resistance, not Moscow. Eventually arms control talks were all overtaken by events when the Warsaw Pact and later the Soviet Union came apart. It was a whole new ballgame.

GLITMAN: I felt that U.S. SDI deployments were not a particular threat to the Soviet INF missiles, so the link between SDI and INF was not as salient as that between SDI and Strategic Offensive Forces. It would therefore be difficult for us to explain to our

NATO allies why an INF agreement was being held up for lack of an agreement on SDI.

The problem here was that we could not and certainly could not be seen as trading off something which was of interest to our allies in the INF area, in order to get something in the strategic side. This would be seen as our leaving them in the lurch, so to speak, and would have enormous political repercussions. So it seemed to me that we really needed to try our best to see if we could not work out a separate arrangement for INF; without having INF held up because of this back and forth on the SDI and strategic side.

The problem for INF, however, was that it really didn't fit neatly into this package. There was obviously some relationship because of the overlaying ranges between INF systems and strategic systems, but essentially they did serve different purposes. It was particularly true of the Soviet SS-20.

What made it such a politically charged weapon was the fact that from its normal bases, where Soviets were placing them, it really could not strike the U.S. proper. If they put them in a base way up north they could, but from where they were putting them, they couldn't strike the U.S., maybe just the corner of Alaska, but essentially not reach too deeply into the U.S. But they could strike Europe and much of Asia. If you look at some of the charts we had prepared to show the range arcs from the SS-20s, a fairly high percentage of human beings were in the range of those weapons.

HARRISON: Verification was always an issue in these negotiations. We had never seen an SS-20. How would we know how many were being produced? The solution was to station observers at the portals of production facilities to count them. But the missiles came out of the factories in canisters—not just the SS-20's, but other missiles as well. Even if we had observers counting canisters, how would we know what was inside? Of course, we could have them opened, but then we would see other missiles that the Soviets wanted to keep secret and weren't covered by the agreement.

The solution was to image them electronically. But then, how should the imaging device be configured so as not to compromise details of other missiles? In other words, what was the minimal imaging needed to ensure that we were counting intermediate range missiles.

Since all these processes would be reciprocal—the Soviets would also have observers at our factories, and would be imaging our missile canisters—this was a very fraught issue for the Joint Chiefs. It required a President decision. But no one thought Reagan actually made it. Bob Linhard had tested the bureaucratic waters, crafted language that nobody liked but everyone could live with, and that was the guidance we all received.

Of course, Linhard operated under real constraints. This was the era of Shultz and Weinberg at State and Defense and they had an unhappy relationship. Linhard couldn't directly cross either of them.

At the same time, there was the general disinclination to involve Reagan in the details—a disinclination that, I'm convinced, Reagan shared. That gave Linhard maneuvering room which he used with great deftness and intelligence. As a bureaucratic situation, it suited me very well, because you could accomplish a great deal.

The outcome was the INF treaty. We never were able to solve some of the strategic arms limitation problems, but we made progress and success would come later. We pretty much put the stake through the heart of Mutual Balanced Force Reductions (MBFR) with the Soviets: the Soviets would never agree on asymmetric reductions on conventional forces, so that negotiation never got anywhere. The INF treaty was the central achievement, and one of the hallmarks of what became the US-Russian relationship after the demise of the old USSR.

MERRILL: Disgraceful though it is, we have since spent nearly $50 billion so far on the SDI program at roughly $3 billion per year or about 1% of the defense budget. Not much in percentage terms but a lot in real terms.

We have gotten something for it but nowhere near what we could and should have. This is principally because much of the research has been constrained by a narrow legal interpretation of the ABM treaty. There's not much point in researching things that are said to be illegal and less point in arguing over it with irrational opponents of the program. That the research was itself constrained means we wasted a lot of money that could have explored more productive areas. In the end the technology leads toward using space and new physical principles and away from a single ground-based point defense.

Shooting Down the Star Wars Myth

Pavel Podvig

The viewpoint that the Strategic Defense Initiative was not only foolhardy but did not bring a positive change in American-Soviet relations is espoused here by author Pavel Podvig, a physicist trained at the Moscow Institute of Physics and Technology who works on the Russian nuclear arsenal, US-Soviet relations, and nonproliferation. Podvig, who headed the Russian Strategic Nuclear Forces Research Project in 1995, claims that SDI brought about changes in American philosophy that have played a negative role in establishing positive relations and taking steps forward toward reducing and eliminating nukes on both sides.

It has been 30 years since US President Ronald Reagan called for development of a missile defense system that was supposed to make nuclear weapons "impotent and obsolete." The Strategic Defense Initiative (SDI) launched by Reagan's famous "Star Wars" speech in March 1983 has survived to the present day, but with ever-lower expectations. Long gone is the vision of a missile defense system that could "counter the awesome Soviet missile threat." That has been replaced with the hope that a few dozen interceptors with a spotty test record will protect the United States from an attack by a few nonexistent missiles from North Korea or Iran. What has not changed is the controversy that surrounds missile defense and its role in the nuclear age.

"Shooting Down the Star Wars Myth," by Pavel Podvig, Bulletin of the Atomic Scientists. Reprinted by Permission.

SDI shaped the waning years of the Cold War and set in motion developments that still dominate—and indeed poison—efforts to stop the spread of nuclear weapons. A program as ambitious and politically charged as SDI was bound to create a rich mythology, and in fact quite a bit of misinformation from its early days still persists. One reason: Until quite recently, almost no one had a good picture of the Soviet side of the story. Most of the Soviet memoirs and testimonies were quite ambiguous and left plenty of room for ideologically driven interpretation.

The situation changed after researchers gained access to Soviet archival documents from the time. David Hoffman first described them in his prize-winning book *The Dead Hand*, which questioned the role of SDI in ending the Cold War. I also undertook a detailed and technical look at the documents in an attempt to reconstruct the Soviet response to SDI. As I conclude in a new working paper, far from hastening the arrival of a more peaceful era, Star Wars made the transition from arms race to nuclear disarmament much more difficult that it needed to be.

One common misperception holds that Washington's advanced missile defense system helped bring Moscow to the negotiating table and make it agree to dramatic reductions in its nuclear arsenal. Indeed, at the Reykjavik summit in 1986 between Reagan and Soviet leader Mikhail Gorbachev, Gorbachev appeared willing to surrender the Soviet ballistic missile force (and agree to complete nuclear disarmament) in exchange for limits on US missile defense. The deal fell through when Reagan refused to give up his favorite program.

But while this episode is often presented as proof that the Soviet Union feared Star Wars would give the United States superiority in the nuclear arms race, the documents show that Gorbachev insisted on curbing the program for different reasons. He was serious about ending the arms race and reducing nuclear arsenals, but he could not get any support for this position inside the Soviet bureaucracy. The Soviet defense industry was telling him there was no way the Soviet Union could agree to any reductions as long as SDI remained in place. Moreover, the Soviet military-industrial complex was quite enthusiastic about the United States taking the lead on missile defense, as this allowed it to reinvigorate its own similar projects—a massive program along these lines was approved in July 1985. By trying to get the United States to negotiate on SDI, Gorbachev in effect tried to get US help in restraining his own military-industrial complex, with the hopes of moving to the nuclear reductions he really wanted. Instead he found that US politicians and military officials were every bit as rigid as their Soviet counterparts.

The archival documents also help dispel the notion that the Star Wars program pushed the Soviet Union closer to the brink of an economic collapse. No one would argue that the Soviet economy was in good shape, and military spending was one of the factors dragging it down. But the cost of the arms race was very far down the Soviet leadership's list of concerns at the time of the Reykjavik summit. Rather, it was the danger of a continuing nuclear buildup that motivated Gorbachev and his advisers to seek negotiated weapons reductions. While the Soviet Union did have a plan to respond to SDI with a similar program of its own, the documents show that work on that plan wound down long before the Soviet leaders came to appreciate the expense associated with missile defense.

US missile defense was never really an effective economic stressor on the Soviets—according to their estimates, technical counter-measures to defeat missile defenses would have cost no more than five percent of their SDI-like program. With these estimates in hand by the summer of 1987, the Soviet leadership felt confident that it could drop its opposition to Star Wars and go ahead with treaty negotiations and later disarmament talks. Although SDI remained a contentious political issue for many more years, the documents show that the Soviets did not believe it posed a danger to their nuclear forces, even after significant reductions in their arsenal.

Finally, the Soviet documents very clearly demonstrate the fallacy of the "dissuasion" argument advanced by American missile defense proponents. One of the ideas that emerged from the Star Wars debate and still circulates involves introducing uncertainty into calculations about the potential effectiveness of ballistic missiles. By creating such uncertainty, this argument goes, SDI demonstrated to the Russians that investing in missiles was futile. Instead, Star Wars had exactly the opposite effect. Far from being dissuaded from investing in missiles, the Soviet Union launched a number of projects in the mid-1980s that were designed to build new and better intercontinental ballistic missiles (ICBMs) that would be able to counter an SDI-like system.

In the end, the Strategic Defense Initiative proved to be a major distraction that undermined nuclear disarmament efforts every step of the way. It failed in almost every one of its missions: It never produced anything that would resemble a workable defense system, it was counterproductive as a bargaining chip, and it did not bring the end of the Cold War any closer. Where it succeeded was in creating the illusion that missile defense is somehow an answer to the security problems of the nuclear world. It is not, although it might take another 30 years for politicians to admit this.

To Dream What Is Not an Impossible Dream?

Gareth Evans

The idealistic view that disarmament can be achieved is presented in a realistic way in the following viewpoint by activist Gareth Evans, who has served as Australia's foreign minister, head of the International Crisis Group, and a member or chair of many commissions and panels on the subject of nuclear nonproliferation. Evans brought forth the following ideas as a visiting professorship lecturer in statecraft and diplomacy in 2013. Though he claims that no international issue has provided a greater challenge, he believes that the elimination of nuclear weapons from the face of the earth can be achieved through goodwill, a brighter spotlight placed on the issue globally, and determination.

O f all the international policy issues with which I have been involved over the last twenty-five years—as Australia's foreign minister; as head of the International Crisis Group; and as initiator, member or chair of a number of blue-ribbon commissions and panels—none has tested my optimism more than nuclear disarmament. An issue that in earlier decades mobilized hundreds of thousands of activists all over the world, and on which every political leader and senior policymaker had to have some kind of an opinion, now barely resonates at all with policymakers or publics, except when there is an occasional flurry of anxiety as to what a North Korea or Iran might be up to. Progress on disarmament has been, as a result, glacial, and shows no signs of moving faster

"Eliminating Nuclear Weapons: An Impossible Dream?" by the Honorable Gareth Evans, May 13, 2013, http://www.gevans.org/speeches/speech514.html. Reprinted by Permission.

any time soon. Nine nuclear-armed states share the current global nuclear weapons stockpile of just under 18,000 weapons, with a combined destructive capacity between them equivalent to nearly 120,000 Hiroshima-sized bombs. The United States and Russia, who together hold 95 per cent of these warheads, have been downsizing their arsenals, but in neither case with any intention of getting even close to zero. France and the UK, now with 300 and 225 warheads respectively, have made modest reductions in their arsenals, from much lower starting points, which will continue at least in the case of the UK, but neither has shown any more enthusiasm than the big two for moving to actual elimination.

Israel, with its 80 or so warheads, though it does not admit to its nuclear-armed status, can be presumed to think likewise. And the four Asian nuclear-armed states—China (with some 240 warheads), India and Pakistan (with around 100 each) and, we have to now add, North Korea (with less than 10)—have been actually *increasing* their arsenals, albeit again from low bases as compared with the U.S. and Russia, with no evident willingness at all to reverse course.

Part of the reason for the non-resonance of the issue and general inaction seems to be complacency: the perception that in the post Cold War world nuclear stockpiles are not the threat they may once have been. Another part of the explanation appears to be an ingrained fatalism: the perception that nuclear weapons cannot be uninvented, are always going to be with us, and that there is little point in playing Don Quixote. But perhaps the most important part of the explanation for government inaction is the tenacious perception in many quarters that disarmament is actually undesirable—because nuclear deterrence works.

All these positions can and should be contested. I am enough of an optimist to believe that if enough hard information and good argument is put into the global public domain; if enough bottom-up civil society pressure and peer-group state pressure is maintained for long enough; and, above all, if enough top-down leadership is shown by the states and heads of government that matter most—and President Barack Obama's continued strong commitment is crucial in this respect—then significant movement can occur. But I can't pretend that ridding the world once and for all of its existing nuclear weapons, and ensuring that no new ones are ever built, will involve anything other than very slow grinding, through very hard boards, for a very long time.

In this lecture I want to explore in some detail the relevant arguments for elimination—acceptance of which is a necessary condition, even if never likely to be a sufficient one, for disarmament. I will then, much more briefly, describe the present state of play in terms of take-up of these arguments and sketch some possible ways forward which may do at least a little to accelerate the process.

When it comes to making the case for elimination, there are five crucial messages that have to be constantly and relentlessly articulated in public and policy discourse. These are that nuclear weapons are morally and environmentally indefensible; that as long as any state retains any nuclear weapons they are bound one day to be used; that as long as any state retains nuclear weapons others will want them, so multiplying the prospects of such use; that nuclear deterrence is at best of highly dubious, and at worst zero, utility in maintaining peace; and that nuclear disarmament is actually achievable.

Message One: nuclear weapons are morally and environmentally indefensible. Nuclear weapons are simply the most indiscriminately inhumane devices ever invented—shocking in the extent of the devastation they cause; shocking in their total inability to distinguish between combatants and non-combatants, between young and old, between victims and those trying to help them; and shocking in the longevity of their human impact. As the International Court of Justice determined, for all these reasons, their threat or use "would generally be contrary to the rules of international law …and in particular the principles and rules of humanitarian law."

It is not just the countless men, women and children who would be vaporized, crushed, baked, boiled or irradiated to death in any nuclear war. The wider environmental impacts are similarly shocking, with even a notionally contained regional nuclear conflict having the potential to cause mass starvation worldwide. A limited nuclear exchange between India and Pakistan in which each side attacked the other's cities with 50 comparatively low-yield Hiroshima-sized weapons is not a totally implausible scenario given the history of war-fighting between these two states and the size of each side's stockpile. And this, in addition to the devastation caused in each of them, would throw up enough concentrations of soot into the stratosphere, which would remain there long enough—a decade or more—to cause unprecedented climate cooling worldwide (the "global winter" effect) with major impacts as a result on global agriculture (the "nuclear famine" effect), putting at risk, on at least one well-informed estimate, the lives of nearly one billion people. [1]

Message Two: So long as any state retains nuclear weapons, they are bound one day to be used. The most serious risk with nuclear weapons is not so much deliberate, aggressive first use by state actors: no nuclear-armed, or putatively nuclear-armed, state (and I include both North Korea and Iran in this assessment) is likely—other than in a situation of extreme, existential threat to its existence—to break the international normative taboo against the aggressive use, or threat of use, of such weapons which I described in the first lecture in this series. Nor is there a high risk, although it is certainly not negligible, that non-state terrorist actors will steal or buy existing weapons or manufacture new ones: the huge attention paid to nuclear security since 9/11 has resulted in more stringent internal measures in nearly all relevant countries and much more international cooperation in intelligence, prevention and enforcement.

The greatest risk from the existing nuclear weapons—and this is in fact much bigger than publics and policymakers tend to assume—is their accidental or panicked use as a result of the ever-present potential for human error, system error, or misjudgment under stress. Most people have no conception of either the size or vulnerability of the current global nuclear stockpile. Of the 18,000 warheads in existence (9,000 Russian, 8,000 U.S., with 1,000 for the other nuclear-armed states combined), nearly 5,000 remain operationally deployed, and—extraordinarily in a world where the Cold War ended more than twenty years ago— some 2,000 U.S. and Russian weapons remain on dangerously high alert, ready to be launched on warning in the event of a perceived attack, within a decision window for each President of four to eight minutes.

Nuclear deterrence may or may not be useful in maintaining the peace: I will argue in a moment that it is not, but there is much continuing dispute about that. The point to be made for now is not about its utility but its *fragility* as a safeguard of anything. For a start, it depends on rational actors on both sides, each making rational judgments about the risk factors involved—and the presumption seems to be, as Hedley Bull once famously put it, that a rational strategic man in this context is one "who on further acquaintance reveals himself as a university professor of unusual intellectual subtlety".[2] It simply cannot be assumed, in the stress of a real time crisis, that that kind of rationality will always prevail.

Then add to the endemic risk not only of human error or misjudgment under stress, the risks of miscommunication—here now compounded by the sophistication of new generation cyber weapons—and of basic system error, with harmless events being read by the systems in question as threatening. We have been much closer to catastrophe in the past than most people know. Over the years technical glitches have triggered real-time alerts; demonstration tapes of incoming missiles have been confused for the real thing; and communications satellite launches have been mistaken for weapons launches (as for example as late as 1995, when Russia's President Yeltsin was told that a Norwegian scientific rocket launch was in fact an incoming U.S. nuclear missile).

As Cold War archives are opened, ever more horror stories are revealed. They come in all shapes and sizes but it is hard to beat this one from the Cuban missile crisis in October 1962. We now know what we did not then: that nuclear warheads were not just on their way by sea to Cuba, but were actually already installed in significant numbers on land—and in Soviet submarines cruising local waters. When one such boat came too close to a warning depth charge from a blockading U.S. naval ship, the Soviet commander, not knowing whether war had broken out or not, had to decide whether to launch his nuclear torpedo at the nearest available target (the carrier USS Randolf). In such a situation, under threat and out of communication with Moscow, he was empowered to do so—with the consent of his political officer. Who agreed. But the commander of the four-boat fleet happened also to be aboard that particular submarine, and he had the power to override the two officers. So it was, by a one-to-two minority vote, that World War III was avoided. [3]

Given what we now know about how many times the supposedly very sophisticated command and control systems of the Cold War years were strained by mistakes and false alarms, human error and human idiocy; given what we know about how much less sophisticated are the command and control systems of some of the newer nuclear-armed states; and given what we both know and can guess about how much more sophisticated and capable cyber offence will be of overcoming cyber defence in the years ahead, it is not the quality of systems or statesmanship that led us to avoid a nuclear weapons catastrophe for so long, but sheer dumb luck—and it is utterly wishful thinking to believe that our Cold War luck can continue in perpetuity.

Message Three: So long as any state has nuclear weapons others will want them—and if more states get them, all the problems I have just described will be further multiplied. There is a long agenda of measures that need to be taken to strengthen the existing non-proliferation treaty (NPT) regime, including universal adoption of a safeguards regime which allows nuclear inspectors to be not just accountants, mechanically recording the flow of sensitive materials through power plants, but real *detectives*, chasing up leads about undeclared facilities and weapons programs. Necessary measures also include effective penalties for non-compliance with, or withdrawal from, the NPT; strengthened export controls; and acceptance of multinational nuclear fuel supply arrangements. But unless the non-nuclear armed states perceive the nuclear-armed states to be making serious moves toward genuine disarmament, none of these necessary measures are any more likely to take wing in the future than they have in the past.

The core message to every one of the existing nuclear-armed states must be this: If you are serious about non-proliferation, as you all claim to be, and sincerely want to prevent others from joining your club, you cannot keep justifying the possession of nuclear weapons as a means of protection for yourselves or your allies against other weapons of mass destruction, especially biological weapons, or against conventional weapons. All the world hates a hypocrite, and in arms control as in life generally, demanding that others do as you say is not nearly as compelling as asking them to do as you do.

Message Four. Nuclear deterrence is at best of highly dubious, and at worst of zero, utility in maintaining stable peace. This goes to the heart of the case for nuclear weapons elimination, but is difficult to sell because so many policymakers instinctively disbelieve it. There remains a very widespread perception that nuclear deterrence actually works, that it is of real value to the national security of nuclear-armed states and their allies, and that its benefits outweigh any possible costs—and that for these reasons no more than lip service should be made to disarmament.

But all the main arguments in favour of nuclear deterrence have, on closer examination, nothing like the force they usually seen to possess. And this is true whether the context involves major-power adversaries of roughly comparable size and resources (as with the classic dyads of U.S.-Russia and U.S.-China); or "extended nuclear deterrence," where a major nuclear armed state extends the retaliatory protection of its own nuclear arsenal to allied states (as with the U.S. and its non-nuclear NATO and Asian allies); or, where a state of unequally small size and resources as compared to one or more notional adversaries, acquires or retains nuclear weapons with the object of raising the other's pain threshold at least high enough to ensure that would-be regime changers, territory-acquirers or punishers would think again (as with North Korea).

In all of this one should not confuse nuclear deterrence with deterrence generally. There are many contexts in which credible deterrence will be crucial in maintaining peace and stability, or other unhappy outcomes. I, for one, have argued constantly for a number of years that a mix of deterrence, containment and keeping the door open for negotiations is the right policy combination to embrace in relation to the world's anxieties about both North Korea and Iran. And I have no doubt that the U.S. willingness to hold its protective umbrella over South Korea and Japan has been, and will continue to be, critically important in discouraging them from joining the ranks of the nuclear proliferators. But effective deterrence simply does not have to involve the threat of use of nuclear weapons. Extended deterrence, in the context of ally protection, does not have to mean extended *nuclear* deterrence. Manifestly strong conventional capability could do the job.

There is a twist to this tale, in that when strong conventional capability becomes *overwhelming* conventional capability of the kind that the U.S. currently has as against everybody else—although for how long remains to be seem—this may encourage others to retain or acquire nuclear weapons as a strategic equalizer: a deterrent against conventional attack. This is the kind of thinking which makes Russia and China reluctant nuclear disarmers as against the U.S., and Pakistan a reluctant nuclear disarmer as against India. But that takes us straight back to the issue with which I now want to deal: just how credible *are* the familiar arguments for nuclear deterrence?

There is the argument, for a start, that nuclear weapons have deterred, and will continue to deter, war between the major powers (an issue that I discussed in the first lecture in this series—whether the "Long Peace" since 1945 has really been a "Nuclear Peace"). But while nuclear weapons on the other side have always constituted a formidable argument for caution, and undoubtedly concentrated minds in crisis situations like the Cuban confrontation, there is simply no evidence that during the Cold War years either the Soviet Union or the U.S. ever wanted to cold-bloodedly initiate war at any stage, and were only constrained from doing so by the existence of the other's nuclear weapons. [4]

Certainly it is the case that knowledge of the existence on the other side of supremely destructive weapons (as with chemical and biological weapons before 1939) has not stopped war in the past between major powers. Nor has the experience or prospect of massive damage to cities and killing of civilians caused leaders in the past to back down—including after Hiroshima and Nagasaki, where the historical evidence is now very strong that it was not the nuclear attacks which were the key factor in driving Japan to sue for peace, but the Soviet declaration of war later that same week.[5] True, the context there was different—terminating a war rather than deterring it—as nuclear weapons defenders have been at pains to point out. But the basic point is that (as one might expect, remembering those psychological experiments I referred to in the first lecture) policymakers can be deaf and blind to risks staring them in the face both when it comes to cutting losses *and* when trying for initial gains.

Then there is the argument that nuclear weapons will deter any large-scale conventional attacks. But there is a long list of examples where non-nuclear powers have either directly attacked nuclear powers or have not been deterred by the prospect of their intervention: e.g. the Korea, Vietnam, Yom Kippur, Falklands, two Afghanistan and first Gulf wars. The calculation evidently made in each case was that a nuclear response would be inhibited by the prevailing taboo on the use of such weapons, at least in circumstances where the very survival of the state was not at stake.

The confidence that seems to have moved some smaller states, like North Korea, to think that a handful of nuclear weapons is their ultimate guarantor against external regime-change-motivated intervention is not well founded. Weapons that it would be manifestly suicidal to use are not a credible deterrent, nor are weapons that are not backed by the infrastructure (e.g. nuclear-missile-carrying submarines) that would give them a reasonable prospect of surviving to mount a retaliatory attack. In the case of North Korea, its strongest military deterrent remains what it has always been: its capacity to mount a devastating conventional artillery attack on Seoul and its environs.

There are also cases where the presence on both sides of nuclear weapons, rather than operating as a constraining factor, has been seen as giving one side the opportunity to launch small military actions without serious fear of nuclear reprisal (because of the extraordinarily high stakes involved in such a response): as with Pakistan in Kargil in 1999, and North Korea in the sinking of the Cheonan and shelling of Yeonpyeong Island in 2010. It may be that—rather than, as the old conservative line would have it, "the absence of nuclear weapons would make the world safe for conventional wars"—it is the *presence* of nuclear weapons that has made the world safer for such wars. There is in fact substantial quantitative, as well as anecdotal, evidence to support what is known in the literature as the "stability/instability paradox"—the notion that what may appear a stable nuclear balance actually encourages more violence under the shelter of the nuclear overhang.[6]

There is a further argument that nuclear weapons will deter any chemical or biological weapons attack. This is claimed by some nuclear-armed states and their allies—in particular as the reason why Saddam Hussein did not use chemical weapons in 2003—but it lacks plausibility. There are a number of other reasons why the Iraqis may not have used these weapons then, including a perception that coalition forces were well protected against such attack, and a fear of individual force commanders of being tried for war crimes. More generally, given that chemical weapons have nothing like the destructive potential of nuclear weapons—and never will, although the future risk factor is higher with biological weapons—it is difficult to paint any plausible scenario in which nuclear, as distinct from conventional, retaliation would be a proportional, necessary and therefore credible response. The U.S. made no nuclear threat against Iraq, and there is no evidence whatever that it would have done so, or would have needed to, had Saddam's forces used chemical weapons. It is similarly inconceivable that the U.S., however else it may or may not choose to react, would see any need to respond with nuclear weapons should it be clearly established that chemical weapons have been used now in Syria.

The weakest deterrence argument of all, although it is still sometimes heard, is that nuclear weapons may be needed to deter nuclear terrorism. Nuclear weapons are manifestly neither strategically, tactically nor politically useful for this purpose. Terrorists don't usually have territory, industry, a population or a regular army which could be targeted with nuclear weapons. And to conduct nuclear strikes on another state, even one demonstrably complicit in a terrorist attack, would raise huge legal, moral, political and strategic issues. If a nuclear strike was not contemplated in Afghanistan after 9/11, when would it ever be?

The more general point that runs through many of these responses to the arguments for nuclear deterrence is that nuclear weapons really are inherently unusable, and because key players know that, even if so many are reluctant to openly concede it, nuclear deterrence has nothing like the power it is commonly assumed to have. Military commanders have long understood that there are formidable practical obstacles involved in the use (and by extension threatened use) of these weapons at both the tactical and strategic level, not least the damage they can cause to one's own side (the phenomenon of "self-assured destruction") and to any territory being fought over. And on top of that there is the profound normative taboo which—again as described in my first lecture—unquestionably exists internationally against any use of nuclear weapons, at least in circumstances where the very survival of a state is not at stake.[7]

So if nuclear weapons are for all practical purposes unusable, and the arguments for nuclear deterrence are so contestable, but the risks of something going wrong are still so high, and the consequences of that happening so catastrophic, why don't we simply get rid of them? Why has the elimination of nuclear weapons been thought to be such an impossible dream? Which brings us to the fifth and last crucial message on my list:

Message Five. Disarmament is actually achievable. Of course nuclear weapons cannot be uninvented, any more than chemical or biological weapons or any other product of human creativity can be. But—like other weapons of mass destruction—they can be outlawed. Despite the evident fatalism to which to I referred at the outset—that nuclear weapons are always going to be with us— elimination is not a fanciful objective, even if it is not, realistically, a short-term one.

Effectively communicating this message means mapping a credible path to zero—showing how it is possible to get to where we need to go. There are many civil society activists who advocate a very specific early target date for total elimination, like 2025 or 2030—like the Global Zero movement, of which I am otherwise a strong supporter. But they have to wrestle with the reality that setting dates which are seen by policymakers as impossibly ambitious—and which, I fear, are in fact impossibly ambitious— seems bound to stop them listening altogether.

The International Commission on Nuclear Non-Proliferation and Disarmament (ICNND), which I co-chaired, argued in its 2009 report that it was more credible and productive to focus on a 2025 "minimization" target—reducing the world's stockpile by then to around 2,000 weapons (no more than 500 each for the U.S. and Russia, and no more than 1,000 for all the other nuclear-armed states combined), and to ensure that by then, and hopefully long before then, very few of those weapons were actually physically deployed, that none of them were on dangerously high alert launch status, and that in terms of nuclear doctrine, every nuclear-armed state was credibly committed to no-first-use.

Our commission resisted the temptation to put a specific date on getting to zero thereafter, because we recognized that the final step, getting from low numbers to zero numbers, involved not just further stages on the same incremental continuum, but overcoming three high hurdles—psychological, geopolitical and technical—as to each of which it was simply impossible now to attach a credible target date. Even optimists have to be honest with ourselves as to how high these hurdles are.

The psychological hurdle is giving up the status and prestige that seems traditionally to have been associated with membership of the nuclear weapons club, especially when it comprised only the five permanent members of the UN Security Council. This consideration—which might be called the testosterone factor—seems to have been, in the case of India's decision to acquire the bomb, at least as important as any anxiety about China. It certainly resonates strongly still in Russia and France, and it's hard to see any other persuasive justification for the UK still playing the Trident game. One can only hope that with the current membership of the nuclear club its cachet will diminish over time, and that the general process of delegitimizing nuclear weapons will gather momentum to the point where possession of them is regarded more as matter of embarrassment than pride. But this is certainly one of the factors that will make the achievement of final, universal elimination very difficult.

The geopolitical hurdle to be overcome is the creation of an environment in the key regions of North East Asia, South Asia and the Middle East stable enough for no country to have any serious concern about at least existential threats to its existence, even if not all sources of potential tension have disappeared. It's hard to argue that condition is satisfied now, or to predict when it will be, but that such a world could be achieved within decades is not as fanciful as it might to some appear—for all the reasons I discussed at length in my first lecture in discussing the prospects for an end to deadly conflict generally. What is important is to not succumb to the argument that movement toward disarmament be held completely hostage to improvement in the overall geopolitical climate: the two developments should be seen as complementary and mutually reinforcing, and properly pursued in tandem.

The technical hurdle is verification and enforcement. Getting to zero, frankly, will be impossible without every state being confident that every other is complying, that any violation of the prohibition is readily detected, and that any breakout is controllable. Those conditions do not exist at the moment, although important work is being done by the UK in association with Norway on verifying warhead dismantlement, and with the U.S. on disarmament verification technology generally, and this part of the problem may well be solved over the next decade or so. Enforcement, however, will continue to be a major stumbling block for the foreseeable future, with the Security Council's credibility on this issue manifestly at odds with the retention of veto powers by the Permanent Five. All that said, no institutional problem is insoluble given the political will to cooperate, and if sufficient self-reinforcing momentum develops behind the whole disarmament enterprise over the years ahead, this difficulty might not loom as large in the endgame as it does now.

[...]

Notes

[1] Alan Robock and Owen Brian Toon, "Self-assured destruction: the climate impacts of nuclear war," Bulletin of the Atomic Scientists 2012 68(5) pp. 66–74

[2] Hedley Bull, The Control of the Arms Race (London: Institute for Strategic Studies, 1961), p. 48

[3] See the October 2012 PBS documentary video on Brigade Chief of Staff Vasili Arkhipov "The Man Who Saved the World," http://video.pbs.org/video/2281376899/

[4] See, e.g. James E. Doyle, "Why Eliminate Nuclear Weapons?" Survival, vol. 55, no.1, February–March 2013, pp. 7–34, at pp. 13–15

[5] See Ward Wilson, Five Myths About Nuclear Weapons (New York: Houghton Mifflin Harcourt, 2013) pp. 21–53

[6] Robert Rauchhaus, "Evaluating the Nuclear Peace Hypothesis: A Quantitative Approach," Journal of Conflict Resolution, April 2009 vol. 53, no. 2 258–277

[7] These factors combine to ensure that the utility of nuclear weapons for compellant purposes is just as questionable as for deterrent purposes. The claim is commonly made that possession of nuclear weapons will enable states like North Korea—or Iran—to "blackmail" its adversaries, explicitly or implicitly. But a comprehensive recent quantitative analysis of over 200 interstate crisis situations, involving both nuclear and non-nuclear

states and both express and implied military threats, found absolutely no statistically significant basis for concluding that nuclear weapons possession, or superiority, is associated with more effective compellant threats (Todd S.Sechser and Matthew Fuhrmann, "Crisis Bargaining and Nuclear Blackmail," International Organization 67, Winter 2013, pp. 173-95). And anecdotal observation very much confirms that.

The Invisible Black Swan

Seth Baum

Few experts are worthier of expressing their views on the subject of nuclear proliferation than Seth Baum, the executive director of the Global Catastrophic Risk Institute, which he founded in 2011, and researcher into the issues of threats to civilization. Baum makes the claim that the unseen nature of nuclear war results in a lack of concern about it from many in the world community. Baum cites the black swan as a symbol of what appears to be impossible and is indeed quite possible. He cites mind-boggling statistics showing the amount of weaponry available to the nuclear-capable nations of the world as evidence of a threat he believes should be given more attention.

Several centuries ago in England, the black swan was a popular symbol for the impossible because no such creature had ever been seen. Then came the surprise: Black swans were discovered in Australia. Since then, the bird has symbolized that which seems impossible but can in fact occur. The black swan reminds us that believing something cannot happen is often just a failure of imagination.

Parts of society today hold the same view of nuclear war that society in England did of black swans centuries ago: No nuclear war has ever been observed, so it may seem impossible that one would occur. Though nations possess some 16,000 nuclear warheads, deterrence just seems to work. And so, especially with

"Nuclear War, the Black Swan We Can Never See," by Seth Baum, Bulletin of the Atomic Scientists, November 21, 2014. Reprinted by Permission.

the Cold War a fading memory, attention has shifted elsewhere. But it is just as much of a mistake to think that nuclear war couldn't happen now as it was to think that black swans couldn't exist back then.

It is true that, in any given year, nuclear war is unlikely, but the chance of it happening is not zero. Stanford professor emeritus Martin Hellman has a great way of explaining the risk. He compares it to a coin of unknown bias, flipped once a year for every year since the first Soviet nuclear weapon test in 1949. For 65 years, the coin has always landed on heads. If the coin had always landed flat on heads, we might think the probability of tails was close to zero. But in some years, the coin has teetered on its edge before falling on heads. Given this, should we still think the probability is near zero?

We have, after all, witnessed many teetering-on-the-edge moments. On October 27, 1962, during the Cuban missile crisis, the United States targeted the Soviet submarine *B-59* with depth charges. Two out of three Soviet officers wanted to launch the submarine's nuclear weapons in response, but launch procedures required agreement between all three. On January 25, 1995— after the Cold War—Russian radar detected the launch of a scientific weather rocket over the northern coast of Norway, and radar operators suspected it was a nuclear missile. Yeltsin and his associates decided not to launch a nuclear weapon in retaliation, correctly guessing that the rocket was not actually an attack. And from May to July of 1999, India and Pakistan fought a war over the Kargil district of Kashmir. Both countries already had nuclear weapons, which might have been used had the war escalated.

Calculating the odds

How does one go about estimating the annual probability of nuclear war—that is, the likelihood that it will occur during any one-year period? It is important to think in terms of probabilities per unit of time. The probability of nuclear war occurring next year is smaller than that of it occurring in the next decade. But the longer we wait, the more likely it is to occur. If the probability of nuclear war occurring in one year is, say, one in a thousand, then there will probably be a nuclear war within the next thousand years.

For certain kinds of events, one could figure out annual probabilities by looking back at history to see what portion of previous years had witnessed the events in question. But this doesn't work for nuclear war. To take this backward-looking approach would be as though people in England hundreds of years ago had looked at their own historical experience to calculate what portion of swans were black.

To start calculating the odds, my colleagues and I studied one specific type of scenario: inadvertent nuclear war between Russia and the United States, in which one side mistakenly believes it is under attack and launches what it believes to be a counterattack but is actually a first strike. We found that the chance of such a war occurring during any given year is anywhere from about one-in-a-hundred to about one-in-a-hundred-thousand, depending on various assumptions. The total annual probability for all types of nuclear war will be larger than this, possibly much larger.

My colleagues and I estimated the probability of an inadvertent Russia-United States nuclear war by modeling the steps involved in going from a false alarm to a launch in response. When alarms are received, they are passed up the chain of command, receiving greater scrutiny at each step as officials decide whether the event in question poses a true threat. Only if the news reaches the top—in the United States that means the president—will weapons be launched in retaliation.

There is some publicly available historical data for how often false alarms have occurred and how far up the chain of command they've gone (other data is classified). We used as much historical data as we could find, but this still leaves a lot of uncertainty. We considered a variety of assumptions about how the uncertainty might be resolved, which is what gave us such a wide range of possible annual probability estimates. For example, it is unknown how often there are false alarms that could be perceived as nuclear attacks, so we considered a range of 43 per year to 255 per year based on data from 1977 to 1983. While there is no guarantee that the false alarm rate is still in that range (this information is classified), the range at least gives a sensible starting point.

Close calls

The fact that no nuclear war has ever happened does not prove that deterrence works, but rather that we have been lucky. What if the third officer on *B-59* had felt differently about launching the submarine's nuclear weapons? What if the Norwegian rocket incident had happened during a US-Russia crisis? What if India and Pakistan could not resolve the Kargil conflict so readily? Accidents happen. In 2013, during the brief period when the United States was threatening military intervention in Syria, Israel launched missiles from the Mediterranean towards its own coast to test its missile defense systems. Russian radar detected the launch. Israel cleared up the confusion before any damage was done, and no nuclear weapons are believed to have played any role in the incident. But it demonstrates the sorts of quirky perils we must still live with.

Likewise, looking around at current geopolitics, it should be clear that nuclear war is no less likely than it ever has been since the invention of the atomic bomb. Consider some of the states known to possess nuclear weapons: US-Russia relations may be worse now than they were in 1995, thanks to disagreements regarding Ukraine. India and Pakistan certainly have not resolved all their differences. China has its individual differences with India, Russia, and the United States. And Israel and North Korea are not exactly at peace with their neighbors.

While nuclear war is like a black swan, though, there is a critical difference between the two: Black swans don't kill massive numbers of people. We can observe black swans and live to tell about it, but the same cannot necessarily be said of nuclear wars. Our continued existence may depend on the fact that one has never yet occurred. Nuclear war is the black swan we can never see, except in that brief moment when it is killing us. We delay eliminating the risk at our own peril. Now is the time to address the threat, because now we are still alive.

Can World Government Lead to World Disarmament?

Edmund A. Opitz

The advent of nuclear weaponry first unleashed in 1945 changed the world forever, writes Foundation for Economic Education staff member Edmund A. Opitz, who believes that the horrific event created a greater push toward a world government. But Opitz contends that the issues are far more complex than that. He offers that even a one-government system would not alleviate conflict between differing cultures and societies and would therefore not in itself create a nuclear-free world community. Opitz offers that much diplomatic work must be successfully accomplished to eliminate nuclear weapons and that any effort to establish a world government would remove the focus from issues that prevent the achievement of peace around the globe.

Wars aren't what they used to be. Men went off to the Spanish-American War with all the excitement of campfire boys on a picnic. Some of them got hurt, of course, and a number succumbed to various diseases. But, as wars go, the Spanish affair was just barely big enough for heroes. One of the heroes of the fracas in Cuba was Theodore Roosevelt, who spoke deprecatingly about the venture. "It was not much of a war," he said, "but it was the best we could do at the time." Such levity was not entirely out of keeping with the temper of the period, but that was three big wars ago. Now, after the experience of the past half century, it is unnatural to jest about war. The next world war which looms on the horizon holds out the prospect of unrelieved horror; little heroism, no glory. Hence the urgency behind our search for any device which gives promise of staving off the impending catastrophe.

World government is one such device, and it has captured the imagination of many intelligent and dedicated people. There are different schemes of world government, but they are alike in advocating a world military police. This gendarmerie is to have a monopoly of the world's military weapons to enforce the universal peace which the world government is established to maintain.

There are many questions of a practical nature that come to mind, such as the basis of national representation in a world government, the kind of charter a world police will operate under, and so on. But these are not basic questions. The basic question is the idea of a world police force itself and the global government which it implies. Is international war due to the absence of a supranational political government which comprehends all nations; and is a world police the kind of device we can rely on to achieve peace?

Proponents of world government often compare their plan to the process by which the original thirteen colonies formed the United States of America under a federal government. If the colonies could federate, so runs the argument, why can't the nations of the world? There are two answers to this argument: one specific, one general.

John Jay provided the specific answer to this question in the second Federalist Paper by saying, in effect, that the thirteen colonies were already one nation de facto, so why not make them one nation de Iure? "America was not composed," he writes, "of detached and distant territories . . . one connected, fertile, widespreading country was the portion of our western sons of liberty . . . . Providence has been pleased to give this one connected country to one united people—a people descended from the same ancestors, speaking the same language, professing the same religion, attached to the same principles of government, very similar in their manners and customs, and who, by their joint counsels, arms and efforts, fighting side by side throughout a long and bloody war, have nobly established general liberty and independence. This country and this people seem to have been made for each other . . . . To all general purposes we have uniformly been one people; each individual citizen everywhere enjoying the same national rights, privileges, and protection. As a nation we have made treaties, and entered into various compacts and conventions with foreign states."

Not even the most enthusiastic world federalist could maintain that the above description of the condition of the colonies applies even remotely to the nations of the world. These are distant from one another, with widely different languages, customs, and religions; full of ancestral antagonisms and often actively hostile. They are not naturally one people as the colonists were one people.

The general argument for world government uses the logic of simple arithmetic: If a local police force is a feasible arrangement to deter individuals from disrupting the peace of the local community, why not a world police to deter nations from disrupting the peace of the world community? The first step in answering this question must refer to the facts mentioned above, which point to the conclusion that world government is impossible for geographic and ethnic reasons. "Maybe it's impossible," comes the rebuttal, "but that does not prove it is illogical." How does one answer the person whose "logic" is undismayed by the impossible? Consider an analogy from engineering, the case of a suspension bridge. In a giant bridge, something like 90 per cent of the strength of the materials is used to bear the weight of the bridge, and only about 10 per cent is used to bear the weight of the traffic. It is in the order of nature that there is no more than 100 per cent of anything, and with the structural materials now available there is a limit to the length of a suspension bridge. It is somewhat under one mile. One may speak of "a two-mile suspension bridge" but it refers to no reality other than black marks on paper or vibrations in the atmosphere. "World government" is in the same category and for much the same reason.

The point may be driven home by the oyster, whose powers of multiplication are such, we are told, that if all the progeny of a single pair lived and bred for one year there'd be a mass of oysters larger than the earth. It is neither the oyster's logic nor lack of it that prevents this from happening, but the realities of the oyster's environment. In a brilliant essay on "The Size of Living Things," biologist Julian Huxley tells us that "size, which we are apt to take for granted, is one of the most serious problems with which evolving life has had to cope." We are not overwhelmed by oysters or other things because Nature employs the "feed back" principle; it maintains an ecological balance with its built-in governors.

Man is not his own law; he is a creature of limited possibilities. Neither he nor his societies can escape the limitations reality imposes on everything. From the fact that a thousand-foot suspension bridge is an easy feat of engineering there is no logical way to draw the inference that a thousand-mile bridge is possible. Similarly, the fantasm of world government has no logical connection with either the theory or the fact of local government.

But this is not to dispose of the possibility of a world police authorized by a coalition of nations. This is more than a possibility, as witness Korea, but is it one that recommends itself to thoughtful people? Some doubts come to mind.

The projected world military police force—unless it frightens everyone into submission, in which case it will be the most extensive tyranny in history—will conduct military operations. It is possible to gain a hollow semantic victory for "peace" by labeling war a police action, as was the case with the episode in Korea. But the peace men want is not merely the absence of war much less is it the "peace" gained by the cheap expedient of calling war by another name. Peace is the enjoyment, by persons in society, of the full exercise of their faculties within the limits set by the equal rights of others.

This condition is easy enough to visualize, as an ideal; it is impossible or next to impossible to achieve in practice—for this reason: Man has predatory impulses, and in some men these impulses predominate. Peaceable men desire to exercise their faculties and enjoy the fruits of their labor, but predatory men want to enjoy the same fruits. There is a conflict here, which well-disposed men seek to resolve in their favor by setting up a police force to protect the peaceful business of society against predators. In order that this constabulary may do its job, it is given a social grant of power to curb predation.

So far this is very simple. But the next question has never been answered satisfactorily: Who will police the constabulary? In other words, what is to be done when predatory men gain control of the constabulary, or when predatory impulses begin to crop out in its personnel? There is no weapon devised for defensive purposes which cannot be used for aggression. Likewise, a police force and an army: organized for defense, either may be used offensively.

This problem of defensive force turning aggressive has not yet been solved on a small scale where the constable is your next door neighbor and thus pretty much under the collective thumb. How much more complicated is a world constabulary, even in conception! Imagine all the weapons of the world melted down and reforged into a gigantic gun capable of blowing us all to smithereens. Who will aim this gun? Who will pull the trigger? It is just conceivable that an American and a Russian might not find it easy to come to any agreement on either of these questions. But it is inconceivable that the very existence of such a weapon would not touch off a struggle to gain control over it. Whatever the label pinned on this struggle, it will actually be world war. Which points up the dilemma facing any effort to gather up a monopoly of world force in advance of any effective public opinion as to the manner in which this force shall be used.

It will be answered that there is just such an effective public opinion in the almost unanimous desire of the world's people for peace, but this answer has to be qualified in important respects.

Peace is a by-product of other conditions; and while many people say they want peace, few know or want the things that make for peace. Moreover, the peace each man or nation wants is peace on his own terms; what looks like peace to Smith does not look like peace to Voronsky. Public opinion on behalf of peace is either nonexistent or too feeble. Where it does muster some strength it almost always relies on wrong means.

How else can we account for this century's deep involvement in senseless war while all the while it proclaims its dedication to peace? Some wars in history have had at least the surface appearance of rationality; the results could be measured by additional territory, slaves, gold, and the like. War is one instrumentality for the attainment of such ends; not the best one perhaps, but neither is it an entirely incongruous one. But to invoke world war as a means of achieving brotherhood, eliminating aggressor nations, and establishing perpetual peace is little short of insane! World Wars I and II produced their evil results utterly heedless of the grandiose official and popular declarations of why these wars were fought.

Both wars received official and popular endorsement as crusades to stamp out "aggressor nations." But the military action in neither case had the precision which marks a successful police action. Each was characterized by the brutal, senseless, and purposeless force that marks a natural cataclysm like an earthquake. In short, these wars are symptomatic of social ills which lie beneath the surface. They indicate that western society is in various stages of disintegration as its main ideas lose their power over men's minds.

The League of Nations was a reaction to World War I, as the United Nations was a reaction to World War II. Both organizations were based on a faith in large-scale political action which is entirely unwarranted by experience. "An assemblage of states will no more produce a universal moral order than a lot of lobsters thrown into a pound will produce a republic of lobsters," William Aylott Orton tells us in his book *The Liberal Tradition* (pp. 238–239).

He continues, "If you pretend that such ethical values as peace, freedom, justice are going to be secured by an international assemblage of bombing planes: then you merely multiply the occasion on which physical force may be plausibly invoked, and invite a perpetuation of that political chicanery of which, this past quarter century, all decent men have had a bellyful. The relation of political realities to ethical values is not one of means to ends. To suppose that the tangible aims and purposes of the great powers will be subordinated to ideal ends by the creation of an international assembly that they themselves will convoke and control is naive in the extreme."

This problem is too deeply rooted to be affected, let alone cured, by the application of external political panaceas. Modern societies lack cohesion. The natural ties that bind men in community have weakened, and the resulting damage cannot be repaired by external patching. A barrel is held together by hoops around the outside; but conceivably the staves could also be held in place by interior lines of force. Only something analogous to these internal fasteners can hold society together; lacking these, society has nothing comparable to barrel hoops to hold itself together. The problem would be serious even if things were static; but they are not. If an irresistible force is exploding inside the barrel, no strengthening of the hoops around the outside will prevent the staves from flying apart. Our society is in the grip of just such a centrifugal force, and although it appears benign, it is actually tearing society apart. Unless it can be annulled, the erection of a world-wide political mechanism to prevent society from committing suicide will be as futile as trying to heat a room by holding a match under a thermometer.

"All men desire peace," remarked Thomas a Kempis, "but not many desire the things that make for peace." Unless men know what things make for peace, they cannot desire them. Without this knowledge they may unwittingly start off on a course of action whose first steps seem innocent enough but whose last step is war. Almost no one intends the last step, but it is difficult to avoid this end if one takes the first steps toward it.

"The Only Solution to Nuclear Weapons Remains World Government"

Some of the proposals to control nuclear weapons when they were first developed, but that never saw the light of day, still make eminent sense. Though, admittedly, they are even more light years from implementation now than they were then. One, as presented via the Acheson-Lilienthal Report and the Baruch Plan, was placing all the nuclear weapons in the world under the UN Security Council.

You can understand the resistance: "Can we get 100 of our warheads out of cold storage? The Soviet Union has been a little more bellicose than usual this month." Another was the concept of world government, which actually gained a couple of feet of traction post-Hiroshima.

For the 70th anniversary issue of the *Bulletin of the Atomic Scientists*, Eric Schlosser (author of *Command and Control: Nuclear Weapons, the Damascus Accident, and the Illusion of Safety*) provides an overall view of nuclear weapons today from, reads the introduction to the article, "worldwide nuclear weapons modernization programs and heightened nuclear rhetoric to burgeoning stockpiles of fissile material and shortsighted changes in nuclear doctrine." A useful survey, it ends:

> Although the widespread fear of nuclear weapons has largely vanished, the danger is far greater now than when those words were written. And the choice between one world or none is even more urgent. Like the spread of a powerful idea, the fallout from nuclear detonations will not respect national borders.

Did you see what Schlosser did there? The money quote: "And the choice between one world or none is even more urgent." He's raising the specter of world government, which ranks, along with population control (voluntary, if course), as leading candidates for the most critical, but also most politically incorrect third rails of ideas extant. Good for him.

Obviously many of our intractable problems, like poverty and the depredations a tyrannical regime, such as Syria's, inflicts on its own people, could be addressed much more directly than in a world where the sovereignty of states is non-negotiably sacrosanct. One day, though, no doubt after an unspeakable tragedy like nuclear war or a mass ocean die-off, we will look back at this time—when there are 195 recognized nations in the world and others unrecognized, such as the Islamic State—and view it the way we now look back at city-states: as a chaotic, conflict-inciting mess.

There is a core of natural pugnacity in all of us, more than likely, and some of us are more adequately supplied than others. So there are going to be brawls and minor riots—which we can pretty well take in our stride. Even a riot involving scores of men, bad as it may be, is a far cry from war, which is a carefully calculated conflict between groups of specially trained men. This kind of conflict requires rationalization, exhortation, and pressure. Occasionally there is moral justification for such a conflict in the matter of defense. When this is the case, the individual does not need someone else to volunteer his life and property for him; he is competent to decide for himself.

In most persons, the desire for peace overrides natural belligerency. So much is this the case that the continuous war we are engaged in must be sold to us as a means of attaining universal peace. How does it happen that even as we declare for peace we prepare for war? To the extent that our aversion to war is genuine—and this is largely the case—it becomes obvious that the war we don't want is an unforeseen consequence of our efforts to get something else. If we analyze our predicament further, we can detect a similarity of principle between the operations of the Welfare State or other varieties of collectivism, and the operational imperatives of a nation at war. We would do well to examine the inference which may be drawn from this observation: that the first steps to war are taken when society adopts a mischievous domestic policy.

The purpose of war, according to Clausewitz, is to impose your will on the enemy, or prevent him from imposing his will on you. In a Welfare State, or under fullblown socialism, the mass of men are guided, regulated, directed, and controlled by those wielding political power. On principle, the wills of a large segment of the nation are bent to conform to the master plan imposed on them by those who believe themselves competent to plan the lives of others. When this occurs in a society as a permanent peacetime policy, that society has taken the first steps of a course whose last step is war. The principle of socialism or the Welfare State has in it, inevitably, the germs of war.

Conscription for military service is but the more immediate application to military purposes of the control of individuals which is inherent in socialist policy. Some socialists oppose conscription but endorse its logical counterparts; conscription follows theoretically from the rest of their beliefs. These people object to the use of a lot of force on foreigners; they advocate the use of a little force on domestics. But if you start doing the latter, there is no stopping place short of the former.

Control merely for the sake of control soon loses its zest. The popularity of socialistic and Welfare State schemes is due to the use of control for the redistribution of goods. Goods can be had by production, trade, or gifts. But other peoples' goods can also be had as a result of political privilege. All varieties of collectivism traffic in political privilege. So do other societies, but not on principle, and therein lies a major difference.

If the producers of a nation are to be exploited on principle by the political class, it follows that the political class can better its circumstances if it has more producers and more territory to exploit. It gets more producers and more territory by conquest. Thus, the first steps to war are taken in the setting up of a system of political privilege as a means of acquiring other men's goods. When men rely on political privilege to acquire economic goods, they have already embraced the near end of a principle whose far end is war.

If we don't like the last step, we shouldn't take the first. In the matter of modern war, the first step is the acceptance by almost all men everywhere, of the false assumption that political committees are competent to run peoples' lives. The first steps to peace are in the direction of a voluntary society in which each person is free to direct his own energy so long as he allows the same right to others. There is no Utopia in this direction, but in striving for a voluntary society we may at least avoid such debacles as now plague our world.

Hence, our dilemma. If we can revolutionize opinion about social organization so that we rid ourselves of arbitrary political interventions in economic and social life, we won't need a world police; if we can't change opinion in this area in favor of a strictly limited government, a world police would either be helpless to prevent war or would itself be the worst tyranny history has known.

Ideas have only one source: the free mind. They develop and spread as interpersonal communication between individuals is facilitated. No social force is so powerful as the healthy contagion of ideas. For good or ill, they will have their way in time against any obstacle.

The only lasting antidote to war consists of extending limited government ideas to the nations of the world; and the first step is for these ideas to capture the minds and loyalties of men. Not only other men, but us. Even in the United States, wrong ideas about social organization have allowed our several governments at different levels to get out of hand. Desire for a world government stems from the same errors which have pushed us off base domestically. There is no recovery save in a changed climate of opinion—no short cut to peace. A world society, in contrast to a supergovernment, is a worth-while objective; but there is no way to attain it except as ideas of personal liberty gain ground and push government into the limited role of curbing aggression.

Chronology

Aug. 1942	The Manhattan Project is established to explore the creation of nuclear weapons.
Aug. 6–9, 1945	The United States drops the only atomic bombs ever used in warfare on the Japanese cities of Hiroshima and Nagasaki, respectively.
Aug. 29, 1949	The Soviet Union successfully tests its first atomic bomb to become the second nuclear-capable country.
July 9, 1955	Scientists Bertrand Russell and Albert Einstein and others sign a manifesto decrying the dangers of nuclear weapons and urging governments to resolve disputes peacefully.
Feb. 17, 1958	The Campaign for Nuclear Disarmament holds its first meeting in the United Kingdom.
Oct. 16-29, 1962	The Cuban Missile Crisis testing the wills of the United States and Soviet Union places the world on the brink of nuclear war.
Oct. 16, 1964	China successfully conducts its first nuclear test.
July 1, 1968	The Nuclear Non-Proliferation Treaty is signed by non-nuclear weapon states.
June 12, 1982	More than a million people gather in Central Park in New York City in support of the United Nations Special Session on Disarmament.

Dec. 8, 1987   The United States and Soviet Union sign a treaty to ban intermediate land-based missiles.

Sept. 24, 1996   Major powers around the world sign the Comprehensive Nuclear Test Ban Treaty.

Oct. 9, 2006   North Korea conducts its first nuclear test.

July 14, 2015   Deal involving the United States and other countries is reached with Iran with goal of halting its nuclear program.

Bibliography

Books

Hans Blix. *Why Nuclear Disarmament Matters*. Cambridge, MA: MIT Press, 2008.

Paul Bracken. *The Second Nuclear Age: Strategy, Danger, and the New Power Politics*. New York, NY: St. Martin's Griffin, 2013.

Alan Dershowitz. *The Case Against the Iran Deal: How Can We Stop Iran from Getting Nukes?* New York, NY: Rosetta Books, 2015.

Michael Dobbs. *One Minute to Midnight: Kennedy, Khrushchev, and Castro on the Brink of Nuclear War*. New York, NY: Vintage, 2009.

David Hoffman. *The Dead Hand: The Untold Story of the Cold War Arms Race and Its Dangerous Legacy*. New York, NY: Anchor Books, 2010.

Dr. Paul H. Johnstone. *From MAD to Madness: Inside Pentagon Nuclear War Planning*. Atlanta, GA: Clarity Press, 2017.

William M. Knoblauch. *Nuclear Freeze in a Cold War: The Reagan Administration, Cultural Activism, and the End of the Arms Race*. Amherst, MA: University of Massachusetts Press, 2017.

Sverre Lodgaard. *Nuclear Disarmament and Non-Proliferation: Towards a Nuclear-Weapon-Free World?* London, UK: Routledge, 2010.

Vipin Narang. *Nuclear Strategy in the Modern Era: Regional Powers and International Conflict*. Princeton, NJ: Princeton University Press, 2014.

Bill O'Reilly. *The Day the World Went Nuclear: Dropping the Atom Bomb and the End of World War II in the Pacific*. New York, NY: Henry Holt and Company, 2017.

Jonathan D. Pollack. *No Exit: North Korea, Nuclear Weapons, and International Security*. London, UK: Routledge, 2011.

Richard Rhodes. *Arsenals of Folly: The Making of the Nuclear Arms Race*. New York, NY: Vintage, 2008.

Torbjorn Tannsjo. *Global Democracy: The Case for a World Government*. Edinburgh, UK: Edinburgh University Press, 2008.

Periodicals and Internet Sources

Anthony J. Blinken. "Why the Iran Nuclear Deal Must Stand." *New York Times*. February 17, 2017. https://www.nytimes.com/2017/02/17/opinion/why-the-iran-nuclear-deal-must-stand.html.

Michael Cassandram. "Peace Education: Nobel Voices for Disarmament: 1901-2001. *Folkways Magazine*. Smithsonian. Spring/Summer 2013. http://media.smithsonianfolkways.org/docs/folkways/magazine/2013_spring_summer/Cassandra_Peace-Education.pdf.

Joseph Cirincione. "What Should the World Do With Its Nuclear Weapons?" *Atlantic*. April 21, 2016. https://www.theatlantic.com/international/archive/2016/04/global-nuclear-proliferation/478854.

Pamela S. Falk. "Opinion: North Korea Attempts Missile Launch as Trump Learns China's Help Doesn't Come Cheap." The Hill. April 28, 2017. http://thehill.com/blogs/pundits-blog/foreign-policy/331182-opinion-north-korea-fires-another-missile-as-trump-learns.

Madoka Futamura and Nicholas Turner. "Teaching Disarmament and Non-Proliferation." United Nations University. September 6, 2012. https://unu.edu/publications/articles/teaching-disarmament-and-nonproliferation.html.

Eyder Peralta. "6 Things You Should Know About the Iran Nuclear Deal." National Public Radio. July 14, 2015. http://www.npr.org/sections/thetwo-way/2015/07/14/422920192/6-things-you-should-know-about-the-iran-nuclear-deal.

Wendy Sherman and Evans Revere. "How Do We Stop Kim Jong Un?" *Time Magazine*. http://time.com/north-korea-opinion.

Websites

United Nations Institute for Disarmament Research (www.unidir.org)

Based in Geneva, the UNIDIR is a voluntarily funded autonomous institute within the United Nations that generates ideas and promotes action on disarmament and security.

United Nations Office for Disarmament Affairs (www.un.org/disarmament)

The UNODA was established in 1998 to promote nuclear disarmament and non-proliferation, the strengthening of the disarmament regimes in respect to other weapons of mass destruction and chemical and biological weapons, and disarmament efforts in the area of conventional weapons.

World Nuclear Association (www.world-nuclear.org)

The World Nuclear Association is an international organization that represents the global nuclear industry. Its mission is to promote a wider understanding of nuclear energy among key international influencers by producing authoritative information, developing common industry positions, and contributing to the energy debate.

Index